RESEARCH METHODS IN CRIMINOLOGY

CRIME AND CRIMINOLOGY

(In 4 Volumes)

RESEARCH METHODS IN CRIMINOLOGY

(Volume -2)

Editor
Prafullah Padhy

ISHA

ISHA BOOKS

DELHI-110033

Research Methods in Criminology

Rs. 2700 (Set)

ISBN: 81-8205-342-0 (Set)
ISBN : 81-8205-344-7 (Vol-2)

Published in 2006 in India by
Isha Books
D-43, Prithviraj Road,
Adarsh Nagar, Delhi-110033
e-mail : ishabooks@hotmail.com

Laser Typesetting at : Shiva Infosystem, Delhi
Printed at : Mehra Offset Press, Delhi

Preface

Criminological research is the systematic search for causal explanations of human's criminal behaviour. It is an ongoing search for the determinants of criminal behaviours and interactions. All research is guided by the search for credible explanation. Criminological research takes human behaviour as its subject of inquiry imposes limitations on research precisely because human behaviour is irrational, unpredictable, and uncontrollable.

Criminological research differs from other types of scientific research in that its subject of inquiry is criminal behaviour. It is concerned with developing and testing hypotheses, classifying and quantifying observations on criminal behaviour, and then submitting hypotheses to statistical analysis in order to say something about the probability of criminal behaviour occurring or not.

The present book provides a comprehensive introduction to criminological research. It discusses various methods in criminological research and assesses the new trends in the field. Students, researchers and professionals of criminology will find this work of utmost use.

Editor

Contents

1

Introduction

Criminological research is the systematic search for causal explanations of human behavior. It is an ongoing search for the determinants of human behaviors and interactions. All research is guided by the search for credible explanation. Social science research takes human behavior as its subject of inquiry imposes limitations on research precisely because human behavior is irrational, unpredictable, and uncontrollable.

Social science research differs from other types of scientific research in that its subject of inquiry is human behavior. It is concerned with developing and testing hypotheses, classifying and quantifying observations on human behavior, and then submitting hypotheses to statistical analysis in order to say something about the probability of human behavior occurring or not.

Relevance of Social Sciences Research in Criminology

The social sciences differ from the study of natural or physical sciences. Social science includes criminal justice, political science, sociology, and psychology. The natural sciences include biology, physics, chemistry, geology, etc. What is the difference between the social sciences and the natural sciences? The subject of inquiry differs. In the social sciences, the subject of inquiry and analysis is human behavior, while in the natural or physical sciences it is those phenomena which occur naturally and which are subject to universal laws and generalizations such as gravity, mass, thermo and aerodynamics, and the like. By comparison, there are no universal laws which govern human behavior. This make human behavior difficult to evaluate and predict.

Behavioralism was a dominant movement in the social sciences beginning in the 1950s. It continues to provide the principal fram of reference for social science research today. Behavioralism emphasizes the significance of individual behavior as the basic building block of social science. Behavioralism and individualism go hand in hand. The Behavioralist studies individual attitudes, personalities, and physical activity, such as voting, criminal behavior, aggression, etc. and then generalizes to a similar group.

In a sense, all social scientists study the same thing--the behavior of individuals or groups of individuals. Political scientists study political behavior, voting, for example. Sociologists study social behavior, courtship, for example. Criminologists study criminal behavior, violence, for example. It is on this basis that disciplinary boundaries are drawn. But the data--the basic observations of any social science, are of the same type because of the common interest in individual behavior.

The method of inquiry known as the Scientific Method. The Scientific Method is a way (a method) of acquiring knowledge in both the physical and social sciences. Science may be regarded as a

— body of knowledge which contains laws and facts that are already known, and

— method of inquiry which claims that science is a set of principles that tells us how to obtain these facts. This is called the methodological approach, or the Scientific Method.

Scientific knowledge is different from other types of knowledge in the following ways:

- Scientific study is systematic or rigorous.
- Scientific study is empirical, that is, it is based on the world of observation and experience. It is observable. Empirical knowledge can be verified and replicated.
- Scientific study is based on the assumption of determinism; that is the search for cause and effect.

According to science, nothing in the universe just happens. Most of us assume that there are explanations for everyday occurrences. If things go bump in the night, there is probably a logical explanation, like air in the pipes under the house.

Scientific study begins from the premise that there are certain recurring relationships, that if Y occurs under a given set of conditions, then X will also occur. How do we know this? We know this from observing X and Y. To base your judgements on observation (facts) is said to be empirical. Empirical thus means objective observation of facts as opposed to value judgements which are always subjective and based on an individuals preferences, values, biases, or prejudices. The claim that democracy is a good political system is a value judgement that most people share, but it is not a scientific statement.

Classification: There is more to science that observation. The scientist takes his observation s and attempts to order or classify them in a manner in which he can generalize about them. For example, if we were to observe different species of trees growing here in eastern North Carolina, we would be able to classify the results into different types of hardwoods and conifers. Ultimately, we would be able to generalize that there are more loblolly pines than any other type of trees. Such is the nature of classification.

Quantification: Quantification is a significant part of classification. Numerous observations are necessary before leaping to generalizations about the world. In fact, infinite observations are required. But we cannot collect infinite observations, so we employ statistics to help us make probability statements or generalizations about the world that we would make IF we could collect infinite observations.

Further systematization of empirical knowledge is achieved by the construction of theories which are collections of logically inter-related generalizations. This leads us to the ultimate aims of science which are (1) to explain and 9(2) to predict.

Replication: The Scientific Method is a method which can be replicated. A research method is not unique. It must be replicable by others who seek to confirm or dispute research findings by conducting the same research again and again. It is through replicability that credibility and probability are established. Replication means that a research project can be repeated by other researchers and their findings compared.

Prediction: Prediction is another important part of scientific explanation. Generalizations allow us to make probability statements about what is likely to occur based upon our observations or experiences. Thus, the Scientific Method of observation, classification of observations, quantification of observations (counting the results), ultimately indicates that some things are more likely to occur than others and thus we can predict with some degree of certainty the likelihood of occurrence.

Types of Explanations

Deductive Explanation: A deductive explanation is one that derives from a general or universal statement. One proceeds from the general to the specific. For example, consider this generalization: All businessmen are conservative. A deductive explanation would proceed thus: All businessmen are conservative. This man is a businessman, therefore he must be a conservative.

Inductive Explanation: An inductive explanation is one that uses individual observation to formulate a general rule. In this situation one proceeds from the specific to the general. For example, a researcher is introduced to a businessman who is a conservative. The researcher based on his meeting (observation) of the conservative businessman concludes that all businessmen are conservative.

Deductive explanations are considered superior to inductive ones. Scientific research seeks to work from theory (generalizations) and therefore from deductive explanations. However, it should be pointed out, that most researchers use both inductive and deductive approaches in the course of doing research.

Inference

Inference is defined as the attempt to generalize on the basis of limited information. Information is always limited because it is impractical, in terms of time and cost, to obtain total knowledge about everything. If everything were known, there would be no need for inference. Since science does not claim to know everything, inference is behind all science, except in those few cases where everything is known about a whole population. It is important to note, also, that inference underlies most thinking, even the unscientific type. In this way, scientific inference is not unlike common sense. Inference demonstrates itself in science at least four main ways:

— hypothesizing;

— sampling,

— designing, and

— interpreting.

These four general areas are sometimes referred to as the "wheel" of science. Hypothesizing usually begins after one has examined the existing knowledge base, reviewed the relevancy of theories, and understood something of the context within which the phenomenon of interest occurs.

In other words, you begin research by identifying a problem area (picking a topic), reading the theoretical research (especially the literature review sections), and finding a research question of interest to you (something that has puzzled previous theorists and researchers). Research questions are longer and broader than hypotheses.

Hypotheses are simply if-then sentences that can be categorized in certain logical forms, such as no difference (null hypothesis), associated difference, directionality of difference, and magnitude of difference. A good hypothesis implies all these forms in a single sentence, and the trick is to express them as briefly as possible and in simple English. All theories contain hypotheses, but you sometimes have to read them into the theories. There's no need to elaborate all hypotheses capable of being generated by every aspect of a theory, but a single theory can generate many hypotheses with its twists and turns.

In the end, all hypotheses demonstrate inference by concisely reducing extant (existing) knowledge into manageable and meaningful form. Extant knowledge is what you obtain from a literature review. Sampling goes to the heart of inference because a sample is what one draws on to test hypotheses and make generalizations. The idea of sampling is drawn from the mathematical discipline of probability theory, and a particular subfield of that discipline called frequentism, which combines inductive (particular to general) and deductive (general to particular) reasoning.

It's the selection of observables to make predictions about unobservables. Sampling, at bottom, is a matter of reducing, of simplifying. Since many phenomena in life tend to follow a normal, or almost normal, distribution (according to the central limits theorem), known mathematical properties of the standard normal curve provide the basis for most predictions, as these are considered estimates of the fit between a sample (observables) and the wider population (unobservables). If the researcher has been thinking inferentially, the method of sampling and the size of the sample will be selected on grounds of parsimony (making do with the fewest numbers as possible).

There is no automatic need for large sample sizes, and the type of questions asked or relationships predicted will, in part, help determine the sampling plan. If one is going to infer causality, then random sampling, or some variant, is warranted. There are both probabilistic (making use of advanced features of probability theory) and nonprobabilistic (not making use of advanced features of probability theory) sampling methods that suit different purposes.

In general, the more one knows about the wider population or context of the research problem, the easier it is to justify use of nonprobabilistic sampling. Representativeness is what one is after with sampling, which means that each and every person or unit in your sample is a near-average person or unit, not some unusual case that would be called an outlier (too far out on some traits or attributes to be near-average). Measurement is a research step related to sampling and the estimates derived from it.

It is important that the sample enable measurement of constructs (unobservables) that are strongly linked to concepts (observables). In general, one should attempt to obtain measures that are meaningful, and this means interval or ratio level, especially if one is going to infer causality. Interval (meaningful distances between points) and ratio (fixed point with meaningful distances) measurement is also related to estimates of validity and reliability of one's research.

Validity and reliability refer, respectively, to whether one is measuring what one intends to measure and if one is doing it consistently. These qualities of research, as well as the general idea of sampling, demonstrate inference by streamlining a project into manageable and meaningful proportions. Design issues depend, in large part, upon the expertise and creativity of the researcher.

What one wants is a good tradeoff between a parsimonious design and one that provides the highest level of confidence. There is no automatic need for the Cadillac of designs, the experimental model (with experimental and control groups), when one can get by with a less grand design. Of course, this depends upon the type of questions asked and relationships predicted. If one is predicting causality, or even hypothesizing correlation (that one thing moves up or down in correspondence with another thing), then the experimental model or a close approximation to it is warranted.

Designing with confidence does not refer to the power of statistical estimates, although there is such a thing as statistical correspondence validity which means that the intended analysis is consistent with the design to be used. Confidence, as the term means here, simply means that the prospective design is one the researcher feels comfortable with and is likely to be appreciated by the rest of the scientific community. This is often referred to as the requirement of replication.

Sound designs are capable of being replicated; each and every procedure is made explicit so that an outsider could come in, repeat the experiment exactly, and probably get the same results. Replication demonstrates, as design issues in general do, the quality of inference. Nothing is ever demonstrated directly and completely. Only by what seems tedious, rigorous, and systematic does more and more tenable generalizations become possible.

Interpreting research is perhaps the prime example of inference. Interpretation is made on the basis of data analysis using some sort of statistic. A statistic is a mathematical tool or formula used to test the probability of being right or wrong when we say a hypothesis is true or false. There are about 100 common statistical tests. A test of one's hypothesis can always reach statistical significance by increasing the sample size, and that's just because the way cutoffs are placed in the tables of numbers called significance tables.

However, there's a difference between statistical and meaningful significance. Statistical significance is no guarantee of meaningful, or social or psychological significance. Generalizeability is what one is after with interpretation, which means that general conclusions can be made on the basis of successful testing of all your hypotheses. There are two things to be wary of:

— knowing the limitations of one's research, and

— knowing the delimitations of one's research.

Limitations are specific conclusions that refer to the making of generalizations possible from what your analysis actually shows. It may be nothing more than the discovery of a relationship. You should always know your limitations. Delimitations are general conclusions that refer to the making of generalizations beyond the limitations of your study. You should always be cautious of overgeneralizing to wider populations; you may go beyond your sample, but not beyond related populations. Be humble and modest in presenting your conclusions.

One way of demonstrating how limitations are evidence of inference is to look at the requirements of causality: association, temporality, and nonspuriousness. These three requirements of causality can be said to summarize causal inference. Predicted relationships should vary concomitantly (association, as one goes up or down, the other goes up or down), one variable should precede the other in temporal order, and spurious variables should be reduced to a minimum. Spurious variables are things you haven't thought of that might explain what you've found.

In the end, there are usually more correlates than causes, and one cannot control everything. Causality is always an inference. This particular type of relationship must be inferred from the observed information, and then related back to known information. Inference demonstrates itself in hypothesizing, sampling, designing, and interpreting. It is the basis for scientific generalization, especially those having to do with the explanation of causality.

It is never the final proof, but because final proof is itself never possible, inference is the best substitute. It enables ways to advance science, debunk mistaken beliefs, and is always mindful of its own limitations. Certain safeguards are built into the process which protect against unwarranted generalizations. The process of generalizing in an explicit and scientific manner is inference.

QUACK THEORIES

Listening to the frequent discussions over controversial empirical claims, an unsophisticated reader could easily walk away with the view that only tradition and prejudice separate the sparring factions. Such a reader might think that most scientists cast a skeptical eye on paranormal phenomena, the claims for homeopathic dilution, the idea that the earth is relatively young, etc., merely because these scientists were taught opposing claims. As one poster's signature would have it, such critics merely engage in "school of thought bashing."

Evidential Flaws

In the foreground of such controversies are the various studies and experiments published in journals or elsewhere. Various professional posters in the science newsgroups often complain about readers who read all such studies and experiments as if they were the same. The problems listed below are a small sampling of the kinds of issues that the critical eye brings to the reading of these studies and experiments.

Subjective measurement: There are unfortunately times when a study or experiment must rely on the measurement of very subjective experience: whether a patient feels better or worse, whether two drawings are similar, etc. This element of subjectivity is notorious for introducing unintended and subtle errors into the result. Studies that eliminate this element as much as possible put the result on firmer ground. Thus, it is better to measure the effect of a medicine through chemical or physical analysis or other objectively measured symptom than through patient report, it is better to compare discrete matches rather than drawings, and it is better to count light flashes with a photodetector than with one's eyes.

Small differences: Studies and experiments that show a small difference between the test and the control when the test result falls within what well-established theory would predict are somewhat suspicious. This kind of result begs for different experimental design, tighter controls, or investigation of other possible causes.

Tighter controls turn positive results negative: If tightening the controls in an experiment turns a positive result into a negative one, this is virtually the death knell for the alleged phenomenon. Almost always, this shows that the positive results stemmed from a phenomenon other than the one the experiment is designed to detect. Future positive results are viewed suspiciously unless a good explanation for this history is forthcoming.

Continuing negative results: Negative results count more against a claim than positive results count for it. This is especially true if negative results continue over time as the alleged phenomenon is studied, even if they are few in number compared to the positive results. The reason is simple. If the phenomenon is real, those studying it should eventually reach the point where they can reliably demonstrate it and where they can teach others how to reliably demonstrate it.

It often takes a knowledge of the field of concern to evaluate these issues. The history of forward steps, set-backs, or stagnation set a context that underlies how a new study is received.

Theoretical Flaws

The flaws above concern a particular phenomenon that is alleged to occur and the experiments to evince it. The step from evinced pheonomena to theory is also plagued by potential error.

No direct evidence: Perhaps the most severe flaw of an empirical theory is that all evidence for it is very indirect. Sometimes this cannot be helped. For example, all historical theories suffer this flaw, since the past can only be observed through its effects on the present. But theories of current phenomena should admit fairly direct testing. For example, if the flow of qi energy through the body and the existence of molecular patterns from homeopathic dilution are true theories, those who study these things should be able to find experiments that fairly directly measure qi and these molecular patterns.

No deepening evidence: Similarly, theoretical knowledge should grow and become more detailed as experience increases. In the 1960s, molecular biologists could only mouth vague claims about DNA guiding the development of organisms. Now they can tell how this happens in more detail, and back this discussion by thousands of experiments that evince these details. Two centuries ago, Lavoisier described how oxygen combines with other elements to release energy. Our knowledge of chemical reaction has increased tremendously since then. But what has happened to the theoretical underpinnings of homeopathic dilution in two centuries? Why does it remain vague mouthings about "molecular patterns"?

Predicted phenomena remains slippery: As experimental and theoretical work progresses, more evidence and more sound evidence for the related phenomena should appear. If the phenomena predicted by a theory remain plagued by evidential flaws as research progresses, then the theory itself becomes very suspect.

Poor investigation of alternative explanations: Often the results claimed for a novel theory are potentially explained by well-founded theories. These alternative explanations need to be investigated, and such paths barred by better controls in future experiments.

Revolution without support: A theory becomes especially suspicious when, in addition to suffering the above flaws, it directly conflicts with a theory that measures well by the same criteria. Using again the homeopathic theory of dilution as an example, if it is true, it will cause a revolution in chemistry and biology that makes cold fusion look like small potatoes. But its evidence remains far too indirect, too shallow, and too slippery to succeed at such a revolution, despite two centuries of research in it.

All the problems above occur within conventional theoretical and experimental investigation. Whether and how they are resolved help determine which theories are accepted and which are rejected. Scientists live on the tension between two poles. Driving them to the exotic is their eagerness to discover new and revolutionary facts.

Warning them away from quackery is a skeptical eye informed by knowledge of the myriad errors that have misled others in the past. Scientists looked at N-rays, slippery water, and cold fusion because of the exciting potential to discover something new. They turned away from these things because the evidence did not pan out. John A. Wheeler invited parapsychologists into the AAAS because he thought there was beginning to be some real science in what they did. Ten years later, he knew this had been a mistake.

The attraction of the new and exotic is very strong, and its lure is so bright that it sometimes causes people to lose their critical sense. And some people, unfortunately, never develop a critical sense. Those who have lost or never developed a critical sense create and join "schools" where quackery is born from weak theories and mistaken notions becoming instutionalized. These "schools" are full of the kinds of rationalizations that people use to justify their views when nothing else is available. There are far too many of signposts, some of them are

"Paradigm" Talk. "Paradigm" is perhaps the most abused word in these discussions. Whenever a proponent of a controversial empirical claim counters criticisms of the evidence by reference to a "paradigm shift," it is time to put on one's hip-waders. To the extent that "paradigm" just means a new theoretical view, it prevails because of – not in spite of – sound evidence.

The rise of quantum mechanics is frequently referenced as the paradigmatic example of paradigm shift. But the discovers of quantum mechanics did not have to philosophically argue their opponents into making a paradigm shift before quantum phenomena were accepted.

The proponents merely presented ever increasing amounts of solid evidence. To the extent that "paradigm shift" is used to describe something about the social and historical process of how research is done, it has little legitimate role in discussions of evidential quality. Most other uses are so vague that no significant meaning can be attached.

The Word "Science" used Narrowly: A quack will often reply that his ideas have evidence, just not the kind accepted by "science." The problem with this is that science is no more and no less than sum total of what we have learned about evaluating general empirical claims and their evidence. With regard to general empirical claims, asserting that there is no scientific evidence is the same as asserting that there is no good evidence.

Quacks want to find some room in between, but they cannot explain why we should accept the kind of evidence in their case that has proven so bad in other cases. In essence, they engage in a kind of special pleading that hangs on attaching some odd meaning to the word "science".

"Scientific paradigm": This phrase has almost no useful meaning. If it is used by someone defending a

controversial empirical claim, it is virtually guaranteed that the argument is bullshit.

Mischaracterisation of the state of the art: Quack theorists often distort the rest of science is in order to make their favored notions seem more equal in comparison. Thus, "conventional" physics is sometimes accused of ignoring the observer. "Allopathic" medicine is sometimes described as based on non-holistic principles, as practicing the notion of "one symptom, one diagnosis, one cure," etc. ad nauseum. This is all bullshit.

"Quantum.": Unless the writer is referring to physics or chemistry, the use of phrases such as quantum, the uncertainty principle, entropy, etc., are warning signs. If they are combined with other words in novel ways – e.g.: "quantum psychology," "democratic entropy," etc. – it is an almost sure sign of bullshit.

Carts before horses: Proponents of quack theories are full of excuses for why they have such meagre evidence of their beliefs. These range from "no one funds us" to "the conspiratorial and established institutions ignore us for political reasons." These excuses would not be needed if there were good evidence for the notions in question. The fact that these excuses are offered is almost an admission that the proponent believes despite a lack of good evidence. It it were otherwise, the proponent would focus on the evidence and argue for funding or institutional change because the evidence is so good, rather than excusing the lack of evidence because of these other factors.

"Millions of Chinese cannot be wrong" : This excuse usually comes in the defense of notions resurrected from older traditions, e.g., traditional Chinese medicine. In some sense, it falls under the "big lie" tradition. In a few minutes, someone with a modicum of historical knowledge should be able to think of several cases where millions of Chinese

and millenia of experience were wrong. The fact is that we have learned a lot about how to perform and evaluate empirical research in the last three centuries and that this gives us a significant advantage over previous traditions.

Once a "school" has developed around poor theories, it essentially halts all useful progress by its practitioners until the "school" is reintegrated with the larger scientific community. The institutionalization of theories in an uncritical atmosphere and away from the larger scientific community almost guarantees that there will be a continuing sequence of "positive" results, sometimes for centuries, even though the phenomena remain slippery, understanding remains vague, and discovery of new knowledge is left to the rest of science. In short, a duck is born. Quack, quack.

Marginal results: When faced with marginal results, scientists will attempt to refine or replicate the experiments until stronger and more consistent results are found. When a researcher spends an inordinately large amount of time interpreting and reinterpreting old data, or new data from the same experimental setup, and relatively little time attempting to get better data, the results are suspect.

Misestimation of effects: Quack researchers frequently misestimate the effects their discoveries will have. While they may speak about grandiose social effects, they frequently underestimate the scientific effects. One example is homeopathy, which would cause a revolution in chemistry if true. Yet the supporters seldom grapple with the idea of these effects. Another example is the frequent claims for a carburetor or other gizmo which will make an automobile get an incredible number of miles per gallon. Simple calculations reveal that the engine needs to operate at higher than Carnot efficiency.

Science as institution: Philosophers, psychologists, and anthropologists, when they deal with science, currently view it as "that which scientists do." Although this definition is possibly useful for what they are trying to study, when it is used as the meaning of "scientific" in "scientific evidence," trouble starts. The conflation of meanings leads to the notion that all those things which any scientist does are valid science. This results into a combination of appeals to authority and ad hominem attacks which are wrongly presented as scientific inquiry.

Analogous theories: Many scientific theories begin as analogies to existing well established theories or as attempts to apply the results of a field of study laterally to something new. Although this sometimes produces theories which hold up well on their own, it frequently gives undeserved credence to the new theories. Well established theories generally apply to a specific well-defined set of phenomena, and the support for the theory exists within that context.

The analogy or lateral application discards the context entirely. The result is a sort of informal belief that the new theory is well supported, when there may be no reason to believe that the two situations have anything to do with each other. An example of this is Social Darwinism, whereby evolution by natural selection of organisms is assumed to work as well to social institutions.

Defensiveness: It is a common human tendency to take criticism of one's work personally and respond devensively. Scientists must constantly be aware of this tendency and suppress it, because unchecked defensiveness is the death of scientific inquiry. When a researcher consistently interprets criticism of his or her theories, hypotheses, or data as personal insults, they become suspect. The researcher falls into the trap of considering it a personal conflict and naturally resists the kind of criticism that is absolutely neccessary to test hypotheses.

2

Qualitative Approaches to Criminological Research

Qualitative methods are used by researchers who are influenced by a wide range of theoretical perspectives. Relationship between theory and research is not a straightforward one. All criminological research is not empirical but takes a theoretical form.

The qualitative tradition in criminology developed in the United States. It owes a great deal to the work of the Chicago School. This school made important contributions to criminological theory, namely through developing 'social disorganisation' theory and their 'ecological model' of the development of cities and patterns of crime within them.While many aspects of their work, particularly, the 'ecological model' have been discredited, they left behind a tradition of linking urban social problems to crime and provided the inspiration for the development of environmental criminology.

In particular, Chicago School researchers focused on the 'dispossessed, marginal and the strange', and included in the long list of Chicago School ethnographies are studies of gangs, prostitution and homelessness. Drawing their inspiration from developments within sociological theory, Chicago School researchers pursued innovative qualitative work making use of participant observation, life histories and documents.This work began to influence British criminologists in the 1960s.

The qualitative tradition is now firmly established in criminology. Part of the explanation for this is the growth of new theoretical perspectives, which are broadly compatible with qualitative approaches to criminological research. Positivism has been subjected to fierce criticism by advocates of symbolic interactionism. As a result, they turned their attention away from the causes of crime to explore the process by which crimes are created and social reactions to crime.

Advocates of the interactionist position see the social world as a product of social interactions, emphasizing the socially constructed nature of crime and deviance.The basic principles of positivism were called into question as symbolic interactionists emphasized the importance of human agency, consciousness and meaning in social activity, and highlighted the plurality of norms and values relating to 'normal' and 'deviant' behaviour. Symbolic interactionism inspired the development of the labelling perspective and the work of 'deviancy theorists' in the UK.

Criminologists working within these theoretical frameworks were anti-statistical.While their work has been subjected to vehement criticism for paying insufficient attention to the exercise of power by feminists, Marxists and critical criminologists, these latter theoretical approaches have continued to support the use of qualitative methods.

Quantitative and Qualitatuve Traditions

The quantitative tradition is closely allied to a theoretical perspective known as positivism, which has been adopted to study a wide range of social phenomenon. Researchers who adhere to this approach aim to explain crime and predict future patterns of criminal behaviour. For Silverman, the qualitative/quantitative research dichotomy is acceptable as a pedagogical device to aid understanding of a complex topic but such dichotomies are dangerous because they tend to locate researchers in oppositional groups.

For some criminological researchers this is not problematic because they adhere strictly to either qualitative or quantitative methodology. While we would identify ourselves as qualitative researchers we make use of quantitative measures where appropriate. This might take many forms. Firstly, it is possible to derive some quantitative data from techniques typically associated with the generation of qualitative data.

It is feasible that a study involving qualitative interviews will produce some basic quantitative data such as counts of interviewees who identified the same issues as important. Secondly,we might use the same data collection method such as the face-to-face interview to generate both qualitative and quantitative data by including a range of questions, some open-ended, others fixed-choice.Thirdly,we might use two different methods, one that will produce qualitative data (for example, focus groups) and another quantitative data (for example, structured observation). The process of combining both qualitative and quantitative methodologies is one aspect of triangulation.

Triangulation can be defined simply as 'the use of different methods of research, sources of data or types of data to address the same research question'. For Hoyle, the term shrouds in mystery straightforward and sensible means of looking at the social world and obfuscates the role of the social researcher. The term 'triangulation' was first used in the context of social research by Campbell and Fiske but was used more frequently following the publication of Webb et al.'s text on unobtrusive measures and social research in 1966.While Webb et al. are keen to point out that single measures are not 'scientifically useless', they propound that 'the most fertile search for validity comes from a combined set of different measures'.

Triangulation as a social science concept derives from a loose analogy with navigation and surveying. The term was used in these professional fields to refer to the use of two or more landmarks to pinpoint a position more accurately than if one were used. Applied to social research, arguments have been advanced for combining methods.The use of different methods can be an implicit or explicit decision. It may also be built in to the research strategy adopted. Brewer argues that combining methods is a routine feature of ethnographic research.

Most research projects in the social sciences are in a general sense multi-method because alongside the main method of choice, subsidiary techniques are used. For example, conducting interviews in a prison will always involve some degree of observation of the social setting, which may impact on the research even if the data are not formally recorded or analysed. Similarly, a study relying mainly on participant observation within a youth centre for children at risk of offending is likely to begin with reading published documents about the centre, for instance bids for funding, annual reports and newspaper cuttings.

Numerous advantages are advanced in the literature to persuade researchers to adopt a multi-method approach, and the overarching theme is that combining methods increases the validity of the findings. Reflecting on his own criminological research career, Maguire argues for utilizing as many diverse sources of evidence as feasible to answer a research question. His rationale is that criminological research often involves working with information that is unreliable to varying extents.

By bringing together different methods with their own blend of strengths and weaknesses, it is hoped that the weaknesses of one method can be countered by the strengths of the others. If the data gathered using the different methods offer similar conclusions, criminologists can be more confident that the conclusions offered are valid in the sense that they are plausible and credible. Similar arguments have been advanced by other criminologists. Denzin also advocates a strong case for triangulation, suggesting that this is the basic theme of his book entitled The Research Act in Sociology. He argues that his definition of each method implies a triangulated perspective.

Denzin notes that the shifting nature of the social world and the biases that arise from the sociologist's choice of theories, methods and observers provide difficulties that a researcher working in the natural sciences does not face. For Denzin, the solution is to recognize these difficulties and to use multiple strategies of triangulation (data, investigator, methodological and theoretical) as the preferred line of action. He suggests that triangulation is the key to overcoming intrinsic bias that stems from single method, single observer and single theory studies.

Despite Denzin's claim in the preface that he subscribes to a symbolic interactionist perspective, Silverman and May both highlight that Denzin's prescriptions can be seen to mesh with the positivist desire to seek an ultimate 'truth' about the social world through cross-validation. In his later writings, Denzin no longer subscribes to his earlier view, favouring a more postmodern approach, which gives precedence to the subjective world-view of research subjects as the only reliable vantage point.

Between the two extremes are calls for 'reflexive triangulation'. This position encourages researchers to reflect upon the fact that social research is not conducted neutrally because researchers are part of the social world they are examining. It also reminds us that data should not be treated at face value.This position is supportive of triangulation but adopts a healthy cynicism about its potential to increase validity and overcome bias. Substantial support can be found for Hammersley and Atkinson's argument that triangulation is not a simple test. Even if the findings do accord, this cannot be interpreted as 'fact'. It is plausible that the results tally due to systematic or random error.

For this reason, Hammersley and Atkinson suggest researchers need to avoid naïve optimism, and resist the temptation to assume that the aggregation of data from different sources will produce a more complete picture. For the majority of qualitative research studies, the goal of establishing 'truth' is actively rejected and multiple versions of reality are acknowledged. Consequently, differences between data are as significant and enlightening as similarities. As King argues, it is incumbent on the researcher to report the conflicts as far as possible so that the reader may also try to form a judgement.We can add here that the role of the researcher is also to explain different findings.

Methodological pluralism—reflects a view of the research process which privileges neither quantitative nor qualitative techniques. It is a position which recognizes that different research techniques can uncover different layers of social reality and the role of the researcher is to look for confirmation and contradictions between those different layers of information.

We would like to advocate that researchers adopt a pragmatic and theoretically coherent approach to data collection, using appropriate methods to answer their research questions. The latter is important because researchers need to guard against the tendency to keep adding research techniques to their research design in an eclectic manner with the blind hope that it will produce a better thesis, report or other publication. A multi-method approach should only be pursued if it adds value to the study by enhancing understanding of the criminological issue of interest. Sometimes there may be little to be achieved by using different methods.

As Jupp argues, some combinations of methods do not work well because they are founded on different assumptions about the nature of the social world and how it can be explained. Hence, combining methods does not automatically enhance validity. There are often pragmatic reasons for considering carefully whether a number of methods should be utilized. Maguire shares the useful advice he received as a novice researcher:'the best tip is to imagine the final report and work backwards'.This should not be interpreted as a rigid approach to criminological research. Instead it requires the researcher to consider what they have been asked to produce both in terms of focus and also length.

Applications of Qualitative Approaches

Qualitative research provides a means of researching the 'dark figure of crime'. The 'dark figure of crime' can be defined as 'the figure for unrecorded crime or undetected offenders, that is to say those not included in official statistics'. There are other ways of collecting information on offences which do not appear in official crime statistics using quantitative techniques. Examples include the British Crime Survey, a victimization study involving interviews with 40,000 individuals aged 16 and over, and the Youth Lifestyles Survey, a self-report study of offending by almost 5,000 people aged between twelve and thirty.

Both datasets are collected from individuals living in private households in England and Wales. Maguire suggests that a 'data explosion' took place at the end of the twentieth century, and he goes further to argue that there is no longer a strong demand in late-modern societies for a crude general 'barometer' of crime; a role traditionally fulfilled by official crime statistics. Criminologists are streetwise enough to realize that combining the different data sources will never reveal the full extent of the 'dark figure of crime'.

More realistically the hope is that combining different sets of quantitative data will build up a more complete understanding of the nature and extent of crime. However, as Coleman and Moynihan argue, there are some areas of criminological enquiry that are difficult to investigate using official data and survey methods. Hence, they suggest qualitative techniques could be used as a means of researching these areas.While these techniques need to be subjected to critical assessment, they should not be seen as a second best or a kind of fall-back to be employed where there is no quantitative data available.

The use of qualitative techniques offer the opportunity to make a distinct contribution by elucidating the contexts in which offending takes place and the meanings attached to such behaviour. One example of a form of crime, which is difficult to research using quantitative approaches, is white-collar crime. The definition of white-collar crime has been contentious since it was first coined by Sutherland, and it remains a contested concept.

Offences are hidden in occupational routines, and for this reason, often the only strategy researchers can employ is to conduct covert participant observation. One example of this form of research is Ditton's study, which he describes as an ethnography of fiddling and pilferage. His setting was a medium-sized factory-production bakery. Croall remarks that researchers are rarely in a position to conduct overt research on the more serious forms of white-collar crime, especially within financial and commercial enterprises.

Levi's study of long-firm fraud is described by Hobbs as 'as close to an ethnography of fraud as we are ever likely to get'. Levi conducted an intensive study of court records from the Old Bailey and Manchester Crown Court, interviewed credit controllers and businessmen, criminal justice and legal professionals, observed four trials at the Old Bailey and interviewed offenders within prison and the community. The latter aspect of the research was limited due to lack of time but also because the places frequented by white-collar offenders were beyond the budget of a doctoral student! Where access to the extent enjoyed by Levi has not been possible, qualitative researchers have been creative in their use of data sources.

In addition to the sources of data used by Levi, qualitative researchers have also made use of individual case studies, investigative journalism, court reports, media report of cases and interviews with enforcers. For Hobbs multiple methods have become the norm,and researchers inevitably have to compromise. Given the difficulties of pursuing this line of research, as long as researchers remain cognizant of the limits of their data, they can help to illuminate the 'dark figure of crime'.

The 'dark figure of crime' includes a wide range of behaviours including corporate, professional and organized crime. Only qualitative research has the potential to provide some insight into these crimes.This argument is advanced powerfully by Hobbs.

> The covert, non-institutionalized base from which professional and organized crime operates favours the use of a range of largely interpretive approaches. Until gangsters, armed robbers, fraudsters and their ilk indicate their enthusiasm for questionnaires or large-scale social surveys, ethnographic research, life histories, oral histories, biographies, autobiographies and journalistic accounts will be at a premium.

Because it leads to an 'appreciation' of the social world from the point of view of the offender, victim or criminal justice professional. Matza first used the term 'appreciative studies' to refer to specific studies of deviant subcultures. This work was based on observation, sometimes involving participation, of the social world of deviants. In this respect the influence of symbolic interactionism is apparent.

According to criminologists appreciative criminology, referring to 'an approach that seeks to understand and appreciate the social world from the point of view of the individual or category of individual, with particular reference to crime and deviance'. In Residential Work with Offenders,Wincup presents reflexive accounts of practice gathered from qualitative research in four bail hostels across England and Wales. The data gathered, predominantly from semi-structured interviews and ethnographic observation, are used to argue that the combination of working with a diverse, often needy and frequently risky, client group in a residential setting creates a unique blend of professional and personal anxieties.

Qualitative research can complement quantitative research in a number of ways. Firstly, using qualitative approaches can help to inform the design of research instruments for the collection of quantitative data. King has used this strategy to conduct research in prisons. He suggests beginning with observation and records, then moving on to interviews and ending with questionnaires. The latter can be used to test the generality of the findings in the wider population. By administering questionnaires at the end of the fieldwork the response rate is also boosted as the researcher has established rapport with the research participants.

Secondly, qualitative studies can contribute to our understanding of the context in which crime occurs and criminal justice is administered through providing rich and detailed data to flesh out the bare skeleton provided by quantitative data. Regardless of the size of the dataset or the number of variables contained within it, quantitative data can only represent abstractions from complex interactions, and as Bottomley and Pease remind us 'we should not allow statistics to make us forget the people behind the numbers'.

A burglary offence, which appears in official crime statistics, is the outcome of negotiation processes between the victim and/or witness and the police. It tells us nothing about decisions to report and record the crime. These decision-making processes can be researched using qualitative techniques such as semi-structured interviews with victims, witnesses and police officers or observation within a police station.

Thirdly, Mhlanga argues that statistical correlations in quantitative research require further explication using qualitative research techniques. Mhlanga's study of the role of ethnic factors in decisions made by the Crown Prosecution Service (CPS) to prosecute young offenders included an examination of case files of just over 6,000 offenders. These files were used to collect statistical data on a number of key variables including ethnic origin, gender, age and previous convictions.

The data gathered were analysed using multivariate techniques, which control for other variables in order to identify the actual impact of ethnic factors. Noting that it is 'always hazardous to move from correlation to explanation' and even more so when the topic of interest is a sensitive one, Mhlanga made a decision to present preliminary findings to CPS lawyers and managers to gain feedback. This took the form of a discussion group.The finding that the CPS were more likely to discontinue cases involving ethnic minority defendants was explored.

The discussion group came up with two explanations for this: firstly, the police were 'getting it wrong' by charging ethnic minority defendants without sufficient evidence, and secondly, the CPS 'could be using positive discrimination' in favour of ethnic minority defendants. Mhlanga suggests that in any further research on this topic, it would be highly desirable to conduct individual face-to-face interviews with CPS lawyers.

Because it helps to inform the development of policies of crime control There are multiple ways in which qualitative research, conducted either by researchers or practitioners, can assist the policy development process. Research can fulfil the role of evaluating current policy. It may also serve as an instrument for generating ideas for policy development. Finally, research may take the form of action research, which integrates the processes of research and action. In so doing, the typical model of academics or other researchers generating knowledge to be applied by practitioners is rejected.We will deal with these issues in turn.

Greene notes that programme evaluations are typically oriented around macro policy issues of effectiveness and cost efficiency. Primary emphasis is placed on effectiveness in terms of quantifiable outcomes. Typical evaluation questions are thus: are desired outcomes attained and attributable to the programme? and is this programme the most efficient alternative? Where possible, quasi-experimental methods are utilized. However, there is growing interest in qualitative approaches to evaluation.

Greene argues that the interpretive turn in the social sciences has allowed approaches to develop, that promote pluralism in evaluation contexts, and a case study methodological orientation with an accompanying reliance on qualitative methods. These approaches seek to enhance contextualized understanding for stakeholders closest to the programme. For example, an intepretivist evaluation of an offending behaviour programme would focus on the perspectives of offenders, probation staff delivering the programme and assistant chief officers with responsibility for managing such programmes.The methods of choice would most likely be observation, interviews and documentary research.

Qualitative researchers vary in their attempts to influence crime policies but almost all research produces policy implications, even if they are not made explicit by the researcher.The extent to which the policy suggestions are taken on board by policy-makers has been the subject of considerable debate.

Action research first developed in the US and the UK in the late 1940s by social scientists who advocated closer ties between social theory and solving immediate social problems. It is typically associated with small-scale research studies. Action research can be perceived as a cyclical process. To begin the process, critical reflection on professional practice is required to identify a problem, which is then researched and the findings are translated into a plan for change.The plan is then implemented and evaluated. The ideal is that the process is ongoing with a rolling programme of research. The reality is that action research often involves discrete, one-off pieces of research.

Action researchers are not limited to qualitative techniques but can use different techniques for data collection. However, qualitative methods are particularly suited to exploratory, small-scale studies.

Qualitative research has a long and distinguished history in the social sciences, arising in part from dissatisfaction with quantitative approaches. The ethnographic studies conducted by the Chicago School in the 1920s and 1930s established the importance of qualitative research for the study of crime and deviance.

Defining criminology as a discipline with an emphasis on empirically grounded, scientific study, Garland proposes that criminology grew out of a convergence between a governmental project and a Lombrosian project. Defining criminology as a discipline with an emphasis on empirically grounded, scientific study, Garland proposes that criminology grew out of a convergence between a governmental project and a Lombrosian project. For Garland criminology is 'a specific genre of discourse and inquiry about crime that has developed in the modern period and that can be distinguished from other ways of talking and thinking about criminal conduct'.

Criminologists will no doubt be aware that virtually everyone has common sense knowledge about crime, and correspondingly many ideas about the causes of crime and the best ways to tackle it. However, what characterizes criminologists is that they subject these ideas to rigorous enquiry by conducting either quantitative or qualitative research.

3

Theory and Hypothesis in Criminological Research

Concepts

Concepts are symbols, abstractions, rather than objectifiable phenomenon. Concepts have different meanings in different contexts. Concepts are the blocks from which theories are built. Concepts are ideas, abstractions, that do not have meaning in themselves.

Some concepts are linked closely with physical reality such as chair, horse, tree, book, cold. Other are not. Love, power, beauty, democracy, alienation, national security are concepts which exist apart from a physical manifestation. Researchers usually have some intuitive notion of what a concept means. Part of that at least is culturally derived. They also have a commonality of understanding of some concepts.

If, for example, we wanted to define power as military power, we might determine how many ICBMs, nuclear submarines, attack helicopters, warplanes, and troops a country has. That would allow us to objectively observe and quantify "power". What we have actually done here is to operationalize the concept "Power" in such a way that it can be observed. This is called an operational definition.

An operational definition is one in which define researchers concepts in such a way that they can be observed and measured. Researchers operationalize concepts differently. As researchers, they want to assign meaning to concepts in such a way that we can operationalize their meaning in hypotheses. Here must consider how will collect observable data on a particular concept. So the operationalization process must take place with an eye to data collection.

Researchers must decide what types of empirical observations should be made to operationalize a particular concept. When a researcher specifies the operational definition of a concept, the precise meaning of the concept become clear.

VARIABLES

We live in a dynamic, rather than a static, world. Simply put, things change. As the name suggest, variables are the names of things that vary or assume different values. Variables are concepts that can be differentiated or measured. For example, rainfall can be measured in inches, speed can be measured in knots or miles per hour, weight can be measured in pounds, agricultural production in tonnage, etc. A variable is a name for something that is thought to influence something else.

A variable that affects or causes a change is called the independent variable, usually denoted as X. A variable that is affected or changed by something is called the dependent variable, usually denoted as Y. For example in the following hypothesis, income increases with education, education is the independent variable and income is the dependent variable.

The building blocks of hypotheses are variables. A variable is anything that varies, changes, or has differences. Something that never changes is called a constant.

Variables that only have two extremes are called attributes. In social science research, we deal mostly with two types of variables: independent and dependent. Independent variables are those things thought to be the cause or bring about change in other variables.

Dependent variables are those things changed or affected by independent variables, sometimes through other variables. Independent variables always come before dependent variables in time and space. Variables that have only two categories, such as Democrat/Republican are called dichotomous variables.

THEORY

Theories are, in the broadest sense, generalizations about the world. Examples are, Einstein's Theory of Relativity, Darwin's theory of evolution, Marx's theory of historical materialism, Keynes' theory of demand-side economics. In each case, these are broad, universal explanations that cannot be proven. Theories can never be proven. Theories are utilitarian. They are used until some better explanations comes along and then they are discarded.

Knowledge has progressed by discarding old theories for better ones. The search for better theory is what drives scientific and social scientific research. Theories are used mainly to explain. If they do not explain, then they are not theory. The statement "most businessmen are conservative" is not a theory because it doesn't explain anything. It is descriptive rather than explanatory. Be careful to understand that a descriptive statement is not a theoretical statement.

The importance of theory in social science research cannot be overestimated. Without good theory, there is no such thing as good research. Although research is guided by and based on theory, we also use research to build on or construct new theory.

Sphere of History

If we look to the sphere of history in western society, it is plain that for many centuries the solution to the crime management problem lay in the hands of the rich and powerful. It was royalty, landowners, judges and the like who, in arbitrary fashion, dispensed penalties for crime. Inevitably, the punishments for crime were severe, typically involving public humiliation, mutilation, burning, and execution: in England in the mid-1800s there were more than 100 offences that were punishable by the death penalty. The beginnings of the changes that heralded the development of the current legal system took place in the mid-1700s with the advent of classical theory.

Classical theory

The roots of classical theory as an influence in law are traced in many texts to the influence of two key figures: the Italian nobleman and economist, Cesare Beccaria, and the British philosopher, Jeremy Bentham. At a time when punishment for crime was inevitably severe in the extreme, both Beccaria and Bentham argued the case for the principle of utility. The principle of utility, in which Beccaria's economic influence is clear, has its basis in a hedonistic view of human behaviour.

The assumption underpinning this theoretical position is that our actions are intended to avoid pain and gain pleasure. It follows that crimes are committed when the criminal judges, making a rational choice of their own free will, that he or she is able to act in a criminal manner, avoiding pain and gaining reward. A system of criminal law, therefore, must aim to make the individual's interests the same as those of society at large; that is, neither the individual nor other members of society will want a crime to be committed.

Thus, criminal law must seek to prevent crime by deterring both the individual and society from committing criminal acts by ensuring that the pain of sanctions outweighs the pleasure of a successful crime. Indeed, Bentham held that punishment should seek to achieve four outcomes:

— To prevent crime.

— If prevention is not achieved, then to convince a criminal to commit a less serious crime.

— To reduce the harm inflicted during a crime.

— To prevent crime as cheaply as possible.

The practical implications of a utilitarian philosophy were to affect profoundly the legal system across nineteenth-century Europe. Contrary to the belief of the day, utilitarianism argued that excessive punishment is both unnecessary and counter-productive in terms of preventing crime. The level of punishment, it is argued, should be in proportion to the severity of the crime. The reasoning behind this position is plain.

If all crimes carry an equally harsh penalty, then there can be no selective, differential effect of punishment. For example, if child abuse and murder were both punishable by the death penalty, then logically the child abuser would have little reason not to kill their victim to prevent disclosure of the abuse. In other words, matching the crime to the punishment creates the possibility that punishment can act as a deterrent to criminal acts. Thus, classical theory offers an explanation for criminal behaviour, and proposes a system based on punishment by which crime can be controlled.

There are two key assumptions inherent within classical theory: first, that we exercise free will in making choices about our actions; second, that we act in a rational manner in making those choices. The legacy of classical theory is clearly seen in the modern day legal systems of Europe and the United States. The principle of mens rea, guilty intent, lies close to the concept of free will. The dispensation by contemporary courts of punishments that seek to fit the crime, thereby acting as a deterrent to further offending, clearly owes much to utilitarian thinking.

Thus, classical theory, utilitarianism, and crime prevention through punishment are powerful historical factors in shaping the way society both conceptualizes crime and develops strategies to manage the problems presented by criminal behaviour. The most obvious challenge to the assumptions inherent in classical theory arose as the new discipline of Psychology began to take shape.

Crime and psychological theory

A traditional starting place in the history of theoretical developments within mainstream psychology is, of course, the psychoanalytic theory developed by Sigmund Freud. Tracing the broad historical lineage of psychology after Freud and psychodynamic theory, we see the influence of Ivan Pavlov and B. F. Skinner in the development of learning theory; Raymond B. Cattell and Hans Eysenck in the articulation of personality theory; the movement from traditional learning theories to social learning and cognitive-behavioural theory, perhaps best typi-fied by the work of Julian Rotter and Albert Bandura; and, most recently, the advent of cognitive psychology as seen in the writings of John Anderson and Ulric Neisser.

Now, the point to make about most of these theories is that they seek to offer accounts of human action that are not always compatible with classical theory. To take the obvious and extreme example, B. F. Skinner's radical behaviourism seeks to account for human behaviour in terms of a genotype-environment interaction and has no time for the ghost in the machine of free will.

As psychological theories unfolded, there were two further important developments: first, theories became the basis of therapies; second, the theories began to be applied to the phenomenon of criminal behaviour. Thus, to follow the broad theories outlined above, we can chart the unfolding of therapies within the tradition of psychoanalysis and psychodynamic psychotherapy; then behaviour modification, behaviour therapy, and cognitive-behaviour therapy; and, most recently, cognitive therapy. Of course, there are many variations on themes and the distinctions often become blurred in practice, but most psychologists would recognise these broad churches of therapy.

The application of psychological theories to offer an account of criminal behaviour similarly follows an historical route that closely tracks theoretical development. Psychodynamically orientated accounts of criminal behaviour are to be seen, for example, in Alexander's use of the concept of the reality principle to explain criminal behaviour. Similarly, Healy and Bronner applied the psychoanalytic concept of sublimation to offer an account of criminal behaviour. Most famously, and perhaps most influentially, John Bowlby's writings on material deprivation and delinquency are a clear attempt to apply psychodynamic thought to explain offending.

The influence of learning theory is clearly to be seen in Differential Association Theory, and in Differential Reinforcement Theory. Bandura applied his own social learning theory to aggressive behaviour, while Ronald Akers uses social learning theory in its fullest sense to develop a theory of crime. The application of personality theory is clearly seen in two traditions: Eysenck most famously developed the theme of personality and crime, while Blackburn's experimental and theoretical work clearly makes a major contribution within this approach.

The impact of cognitive psychology is seen in two conceptually distinct research camps. The first approach is to be found in studies that are concerned with social cognition and social information processing in offenders. A body of evidence has accrued on the relationship between social cognition, such as empathy, social problem solving, moral reasoning and social perception, and offending. Similarly, Kenneth Dodge has developed a comprehensive model of social information processing as applied to understanding delinquent behaviour.

Allied to this approach is the influential research by Raymond Novaco on the role of anger in violent crime. Dodge's work is concerned with the interaction between socio-cognitive development and the aetiology of child and adolescent problems, including delinquent behaviour. The exploration of the overlap between this work and the findings of the longitudinal research, as exemplified by the highly influential work of David Farrington, is a project waiting to be completed. The second cognitive approach, portraying the offender as a rational decisionmaker, is interesting for two reasons.

First, this approach applies a particular branch of cognitive research, decision-making, to understanding criminal behaviour. Second, the view of the offender as a rational decision-maker stands comparison with the classical view of the offender acting of their own free will. Indeed, the whole approach of rational decisionmaking has been seen as heralding the advent of neo-classical criminological theory.

Rise of rehabilitation through treatment

Not content with the development of psychological explanations of criminal behaviour, psychologists were eager to turn theory into practice. As the development of treatment methods followed theoretical advances in psychology, so a succession of therapeutic approaches was applied to work with offenders. For example, working within a psychoanalytic tradition, August Aichhorn articulated a theory of latent delinquency. Working from this position, in which delinquent behaviour is seen as the product of a failure in psychological development, Aichhorn developed therapeutic methods to work with young offenders.

Throughout the years up to the 1970s, treatment with offenders was dominated by methods following psychodynamic principles, with counselling and group therapy particularly widely applied. In addition, educational programmes proved popular during that period, a trend still evident today. While treatment within a psychodynamic tradition continues today, the decades since the 1970s, 1980s, and 1990s have seen an upsurge in offender treatment programmes based on behavioural and cognitive-behavioural principles.

Thus, certainly by the late 1950s and into the 1960s, a position had been reached in which psychological theories had been applied to criminal behaviour, and associated treatments were relatively widely used for a range of offender groups.

Conflict Between Criminal Justice and Treatment: It is during the 1960s that the first contemporary signs of unease can be detected. There are three apparent assumptions inherent within a treatment philosophy; that is, determinism, differentiation, and pathology. Each of these three assumptions sets advocates of treatment in potential conflict with a criminal justice system that is configured on principles stemming from classical theory.

First, determinism holds that factors outside of the individual's control-be they biological, psychological, social factors, or, more likely, some combination of all three-bring about the individual's behaviour. Second, the logical conclusion from a deterministic position is that criminals are different from non-criminals.

The origin of this differentiation may be biological, psychological, or social, but the position remains that criminals are in some way different from people who are not criminals. Third, the notion of pathology, the logical next step from differentiation, is that the difference between criminals and non-criminals is one of abnormality. The cause of the abnormality may be individual to the offender (i. e. biological or psychological) or social through learning from an abnormal environment.

Thus, we arrive at a position in which the offender is portrayed as a victim of circumstance, with some level of individual or social "wrongness" or abnormality as the root cause of their behaviour. Of course, it is easy to close the loop in arguing that some form of intervention, be it treatment or welfare, is needed to "cure" the offender of their crimes.

Now, clearly there are cases where the legal system makes due allowances, as, for example, with mentally disordered offenders, but in the main, determinism, differentiation, and pathology stand in direct conflict with a system based on the notion of free will. A deterministic position, in which the individual is compelled to offend by forces beyond their control, does not accord with rational hedonism as the basis for a criminal justice system. Throughout the 1950s and 1960s an uneasy truce existed between advocates of treatment and the criminal justice system.

Social and probation workers would plead their clients' cases, typically on grounds of personal or social mitigation, and the courts would consider a just verdict. However, it is clear that from a philosophicalst and point, rehabilitation and deterrence make uneasy companions. The tensions between psychological models of offending, rehabilitation through treatment, and the theoretical underpinnings of criminal justice can be seen elsewhere in the system.

As the academic study of crime grew, it became evident that criminology, with its academic base in sociology, was not going to accept easily the imposition of psychology and its attendant theories.

Conflict Between Criminology and Psychology: It is difficult to unravel the history of criminology with the myriad of twists and turns that characterize its development as an academic discipline both in Britain and the United States. With its roots in early psychiatric research in prisons, much of it government funded, the first studies in criminology were steeped in a positivist tradition, searching for the essential determinants of crime and the differences between criminals and non-criminals. However, by the 1950s an identifiable sociological criminology had begun to emerge.

The forerunner of this sociological tradition in criminology is generally acknowledged to be the Chicago School and its famous studies, conducted through the 1920s, 1930s, and 1940s, showing the relationship between social organization (within the city of Chicago) and the incidence of crime. The American sociological criminology developed with, for example, the formulation of strain theory, Cohen's theory of delinquent subcultures, and social control theory. With the possible exception of Sutherland's differential association theory, criminology in the United States became predominantly a matter of sociological concern.

In Britain there was some criminological research in the American sociological tradition, as seen in the work of Morris,Willmott, and Downes. However, the late 1960s and 1970s were to see a remarkable intellectual contribution by British criminologists. With its roots in deviancy theory, labelling theory, and European philosophy, the publication in 1973 of The New Criminology by Taylor,Walton, and Young marked the real impact of left-wing political analysis in mainstream criminology.

While of immense theoretical significance, the new criminology was outright in its rejection of psychological theory and research in the criminological arena. Since the 1970s, it appears that sociological criminology has become increasingly fragmented with the advent of left realism, critical criminology, feminist criminology, neo-classical theory, and even neo-positivism. However, it is the 1970s that is the key period as we move from the sphere of the past to the sphere of the present.

Fall of rehabilitation

While the offender treatment ideal flourished throughout the 1950s and 1960s, the fall was waiting to happen. Like a gunshot precipitating an avalanche, the publication in 1974 of Robert Martinson's paper, "What Works? Questions and Answers About Prison Reform", heralded a rush of those eager to disavow rehabilitation. Who were these opponents of rehabilitation? Cullen and Gendreau offer an analysis of the political and academic forces that very quickly quelled the rehabilitative ideal.

The marked political shift to the right in both the United States and Britain resolved the conflict between rehabilitation and the criminal justice system. Rehabilitation had been shown not to work and the return to a criminal justice philosophy based on force of punishment and just desserts quickly followed. In England and Wales, for example, the 1979 May Report on the prison service asserted that the rhetoric of training and treatment had had its day and prisons should aim no higher than humane containment.

The message that "nothing works" was also in accord with the dominant criminological theories of the mid-1970s, which, as noted above, were heavily based on political analysis and rejected the need for theories of crime that included individual factors. Thus, academic opposition to the overthrow of the rehabilitative ideal was, at best, fragmentary and, at worst, destructive.

As the message that "nothing works" continued to hit home during the 1980s, there were three significant strands of development. First, it was clear that any proponents of treatment would be working against the ethos of the day. The 1980s became a time for the implementation of harsh measures, such as prison regimes given to boot camps and "short sharp shocks", to punish offenders harshly and deter them from a life of crime. Second, government funding shifted away from rehabilitation and into situational crime prevention. With its roots in a view of offenders as hedonistic rational decision-makers, this approach was in accord with classical theory and so attracted considerable government patronage.

The legacy of situational crime prevention is to be seen in the plethora of alarms, security devices, video cameras, and electronic tagging of offenders that have rapidly become part of everyday life. Third, the research base in support of the effectiveness of treatment was subjected to intense academic criticism. While all research can be criticized, the thesis has been advanced that the real intention of the adverse academic criticism was to destroy the knowledge that human scientists could bring to explaining crime.

As events unfolded, the 1980s became a low point for those holding to the rehabilitative ideal: all notions of rehabilitation of offenders, including treatment, were looked on with scepticism and disfavour. The fall from grace was at its nadir.

Sphere of the Present

If the 1980s saw the fall of the rehabilitative ideal, then the early 1990s witnessed a spectacular resurrection, certainly in Canada and Britain and also in parts of the United States. The resurrection of treatment as an option within the criminal justice system can be directly traced to the impact of a string of metaanalytic studies of the effects of offender treatment published towards the end of the 1980s and into the 1990s; with several syntheses also available.

The message emerging from these studies was that treatment with offenders can have a small but significant effect in terms of reducing re-offending. Further, when certain treatment factors are combined, the meta-analyses suggest that this small effect can be considerably enhanced. It has therefore proved possible to describe the characteristics of "high-impact" programmes for offenders.

Briefly, high-impact programmes would have the following characteristics: theoretically, they would espouse a cognitive-behavioural perspective; they would focus on the offence behaviour of high-risk offenders; the treatment would be delivered using a structured programme with defined aims and objectives; the treatment would be delivered by highly trained practitioners; and organizations would support, manage, and evaluate the programmes to ensure high treatment integrity.

Research findings need a voice if they are to reach policy makers and practitioners: the development of the "what works" agenda, first by a small group of psychologists and probation officers, then by increasingly large numbers from several professions and service agencies, has provided the necessary impetus for a real movement to be evident. Now, it would be wrong to assume that the case for treatment is proven: it is evident that a great deal more work needs to be carried out on the effectiveness of treatment. In particular, the outcome evidence from current treatment programmes configured according to "what works" principles will prove critical over the coming years.

Sphere of the Future

The resurrection of offender treatment raises some interesting possibilities in both the short and long term. In the short term it might be predicted that service agencies will focus on four interrelated aspects of treatment delivery. First, there will be a continued and growing interest in cognitive-behavioural theory and practice. Second, considerably more attention will be paid to practitioner training in order to ensure high-quality delivery of treatment programmes.

Third, the issue of treatment integrity will assume greater importance, with more attention being paid to the management, supervision, and support of practitioners delivering treatment. Finally, in an era of evidence-based practice, service agencies will develop ever more sophisticated systems of monitoring and evaluating the effects of treatment.

In terms of treatment content, it is likely that programmes will become ever more complex, seeking to attend to a range of criminogenic needs. This, in turn, raises questions about the configuration of service agencies: will it be tenable to have separate, dislocated agencies-say at different stages of sentence, or in custody versus community-when the aim should be coherent, sustained treatment? Further, recent evidence suggests that there are strong grounds, in terms of reducing recidivism, for increasing the application of "Concept Therapeutic Communities" and Milieu Therapies with offender groups.

For academics and researchers there are many issues awaiting debate. While recent attention has focused on the practical implications of "what works", the theoretical interpretation of the research base (mainly the meta-analyses) remains largely unattempted. It is also important that thought is given to the prevailing belief, discussed above, that "treatment equals pathology". There urgently needs to be some conceptual reworking of this issue in order to move the field forward.

However, it is the findings of the eventual long-term recidivism studies from the current "what works" programmes that will undoubtably have the greatest impact over the next generation. It might also be hoped that there might be a rapprochement between psychology and criminology, so that both sides can constructively engage in the study and prevention of criminal behaviour.

Hypothesis

A hypothesis is a statement that proposes a relationship between two or more variables. It is specified as X affects Y. It is a tentative statement about how the researcher thinks the variable may be related to each other. For example:

— Political participation increases with education.

— Union members are more likely to vote Democratic than non-union members.

— People with college degrees earn higher incomes.

Hypotheses seek to establish both direction and magnitude. A directional hypothesis states the expected direction of the relationship, or how the researcher thinks the variables are related. For example: As more countries become industrialized, infant mortality will increase.

A nondirectional hypothesis simply states that there is a relationship but does not specify the direction of the relationship. For example: As more countries become industrialized, infant mortality will be affected. There is also a null hypothesis to consider. The null hypothesis says that there is no relationship between the independent and dependent variables. For example: A country's level of industrialization has no affect on infant mortality.

Magnitude in relationships refers to the extent of change in the dependent variable caused by a change in the independent variable. Never in the social science can all of the change in the dependent variable be explained by a change in the independent variable.

Properties of Good Hypotheses:

- Hypotheses should be constructed in such a way that they lend themselves to the Scientific Method.
- They should be empirical statements; never normative or value statements about what should or should not be.
- A hypothesis should describe a general phenomena not a particular occurrence.
- A good hypothesis should be plausible. There should be some logical reason for thinking it possible.
- A good hypothesis is specific. The concepts used are clearly defined. An example of a bad hypothesis is to say that there is a relationship between personality and political attitudes. Which personality type? What attitudes? A good hypothesis is more specific, e.g., People who feel alienated are not likely to have a strong trust in government.
- Last, a good hypothesis is testable. There must be evidence that is obtainable which will indicate whether the hypothesis is correct or not.

The point is that the more specific you make your hypotheses, the better. Not only may you be able to use more powerful statistics, but you will be engaging in what is called confirmatory research, instead of what is called exploratory research.

The more your topic has been previously researched by others, the more it is expected that you will use confirmatory research. Exploratory research is used only in previously uncharted areas, or by those who honestly don't know anything about their topic. You'll note that the last example above contains all the elements of previous examples, so you can always drop down to a less rigorous hypothesis, but you can't or shouldn't move up to a more specific one after you've already done your research.

Also, the null hypothesis remains unstated or implied as no differences, no matter how complex your other (called alternative) hypotheses get. Technically, all statistical tests are tests of the null hypothesis first, which is rejected in favor of degrees of confidence in the alternatives. An important part of the research process that goes along with hypothesis formulation is constructing your operational definitions.

These are definitions of your variables for research purposes. They are important so others can understand and replicate your research. Researchers need to define their variables very precisely, especially the dependent variables. If "crime" is your dependent variable, you need to be very precise about exactly what kind of crime you have in mind: violent crime; property crime; vice crime; etc.

Hypotheses in Research

The building blocks of hypotheses are variables. A variable is anything that varies, changes, or has differences.

Something that never changes is called a constant. Variables that only have two extremes are called attributes. In social science research, deal mostly with two types of variables: independent and dependent. Independent variables are those things thought to be the cause or bring about change in other variables.

Dependent variables are those things changed or affected by independent variables, sometimes through other variables. Independent variables always come before dependent variables in time and space. Hypotheses are simply if-then sentences that can be categorized in certain logical forms, such as no difference (null hypothesis), associated difference, directionality of difference, and magnitude of difference.

A good hypothesis implies all these in a single sentence, and the trick is to express them as briefly as possible and in simple English. An important part of the research process that goes along with hypothesis formulation is constructing your operational definitions. These are definitions of your variables for research purposes. They are important so others can understand and replicate your research. Researchers need to define their variables very precisely, especially the dependent variables. If "crime" is your dependent variable, you need to be very precise about exactly what kind of crime you have in mind: violent crime; property crime; vice crime; etc.

Steps in Formulating a Hypothesis

— Decide what you want to explain: choose a dependent variable

  — Your dependent variable must show variation

  — Run Descriptives to see mean and dispersion statistics

  - Even better, run Frequencies, and call for a histogram along with the mean and std. dev.
- Choose independent variables that also show variation
  - One can't explain variation in a dependent variable with an independent variable that doesn't vary.
  - Moreover, the variation in the independent must match that in the dependent variable.
  - Otherwise, they can't possibly covary, which is needed for the covariation needed in correlation.
  - Examples of lack of theoretical potential:
  - Voting for Clinton in 1996 in the suburb of Winnetka can't be explained by race, for race does not vary much in Winnetka.
  - Variation across time in deaths in domestic violence within nations can't be explained by ethnic diversity, for ethnicity doesn't change much across time within a nation.
  - However, variation in deaths across nations can be related to variation in ethnic diversity across nations.
- Think of multiple causes of the dependent variable:
  - Do two or more independent variables combine to affect it?
  - Consider using multiple regression to deal with multiple causes.
  - Does a relationship hold for some units of analysis but not others?
  - For northern states but not for southern ones?
  - For European nations but not for Third World nations?

— For whites, but not for blacks?

— For reformed cities, but not unreformed cities?

— For multi-party states, but not single-party states?

— Try to develop your analysis so that it considers all the cases, even if the relationship doesn't apply equally to them.

— Consider alternative measures of both the dependent and independent variables.

4

Life Course Theory and Criminological Research

The subject of life course theory is the study of patterns and variations in people's experiences. Researchers divided the life course into three stages: (1) prenatal and early childhood, (2) early adolescence and young adulthood, and (3) adulthood and old age. The prenatal and early childhood life stage encompasses the time from conception through age 10. During this stage, biology and family are the most important factors. For some children, signs of future trouble begin to appear very early during this period. The second stage begins around age 10 and continues through the teenage years to approximately age 20. During this period of the life course, we will witness an explosion of criminal, deviant, and antisocial behavior.

Involvement in delinquent behavior typically peaks sometime between the ages of 15 and 17. After the late teenage years, crime and deviance start to decline rapidly. The adult stage begins around age 21. During this stage, involvement in criminal and antisocial activity continues to decline, but the consequences of earlier criminality begin to manifest themselves more profoundly in other life trajectories, most notably family and occupation. In the latter stages of life, intensive involvement in crime becomes rare. Those who were most active in the earlier stages are by now either serving long terms of incarceration, or are physically debilitated from long years of drug and alcohol abuse, or dead.

Crime is both a dependent and an independent variable, a cause as well as an effect. Just as there are social causes of crime, crime itself has causal effects on other domains of life. Thus, as we move through the three stages, we will trace the factors that influence trajectories in crime and explore the consequences of following particular crime trajectories on other domains in life. Among the factors that shape trajectories in crime are social class, race, gender, family, and neighborhood context. Among the potential consequences of involvement in crime are reduced opportunities for a good family life and a worthwhile occupational career.

Perspective of Life Course

The life course perspective is a broad multidisciplinary intellectual movement. It encompasses ideas and empirical observations from a variety of disciplines, including history, biology, psychology, and sociology, to name a few. It is not an explicit theory of anything, but rather a new way of thinking about and studying human lives and development; it is an emerging paradigm. In its simplest sense, the life course may be defined as the "duration of a person's existence".

The duration of a person's existence, however, does not simply consist of a continuous flux of undifferentiated time and experience. Life is more structured than that. Our lives consist of a sequence of phases that are socially constructed and that are recognized by individuals and society as being different from one and another. The different phases typically are separated from each other by normatively defined transitions and tend to be ordered in the sense that certain events are expected to precede or follow other events most of the time. For example, from a normative point of view getting married is expected to proceed to having children, even though the ordering of these two events often is reversed in practice.

Glen H. Elder, Jr., a leading figure in life course research, defines the life course as the interconnected trajectories that a person has as he or she ages through life. A trajectory is a sequence of linked states within a conceptually defined range of behavior or experience. It is a career or pathway over the life span. For example, we can speak of a person's educational trajectory, which is a series of linked states related to education. To illustrate, for many people the standard educational trajectory consists of passage through elementary school, junior high school, high school, and college, leading eventually to a college degree and cessation of the formal educational trajectory around age 22 or 23.

As people move through this trajectory, they graduate from one level of schooling to another. Each graduation marks a change in state that is called a transition. Entering college marks a transition from one state to another in an educational trajectory. Transitions are always embedded in trajectories, and the states that make up a trajectory are always linked to one another by transitions.

According to Elder, the life course perspective is based on four central premises, which can be summarized as the following:

— Aging and developmental change must be viewed as continuous processes that occur throughout life.

— Trajectories in different realms of life are interconnected and have reciprocal effects on one another.

— Human development is influenced by social and historical conditions.

— Efforts to optimize human development through preventive or corrective interventions will be most effective if they are sensitive to the developmental needs and capabilities of particular age periods in the life span.

Although we typically think of development and growth primarily in regard to children or adolescents, the life course perspective holds that "aging is not simply growing old beyond some arbitrary point in the life course". Rather, aging and development are continuous processes. Adulthood is not a static unchanging condition. As adults age, they undergo continuous biological, psychological, and social changes, though perhaps at slower rates than children and adolescents.

Aging and development go on continuously from the moment of one's conception in the womb to one's last breath. From beginning to end, we change and develop biologically, psychologically, and socially. Life course researchers typically conceive of trajectories in three different domains of human behavior and functioning-biological, psychological, and social. According to the second premise of the life course perspective, trajectories in these different realms are intimately connected and have reciprocal effects on each other. Biological developments can influence our psychological and social trajectories.

For example, as biological beings, we are born without the ability to reproduce. We develop reproductive capacity when we go through puberty. Puberty is an important biological transition that has important implications for psychological and social trajectories. When young women go through puberty, they often experience profound changes in their psychological makeup, such as reduced selfesteem. Thus, puberty may lead to a transition in psychological trajectories of young women, which may in turn affect how they perform in school and hence have the potential to alter their educational trajectories.

Indeed, researchers have found that in some settings girls who reach menarche at age 11 or younger are more likely to exhibit multiple forms of behavioral deviancy than girls who mature later. Thus, a transition in a biological trajectory can have ramifications for psychological and social trajectories. In turn, social events also may influence psychological and even biological trajectories. Trajectories across and within the different domains of human behavior and functioning have mutual interactive effects on one another.

The third premise of the life course perspective is more complex than the first two and requires a more extended discussion. The premise is that human development is multidetermined and influenced by social and historical conditions and changes. As we develop over the life course, we are shaped by a multitude of factors and experiences. Some of these factors and experiences are close, personal, and very direct in their effects upon us. For example, the type of family we grow up in, our relationships with our parents, whether we have older or younger siblings, all of these idiosyncratic circumstances that characterize our personal histo-ries can dramatically shape our development and the trajectories we follow in life.

Our individual lives are linked to the lives of others in the sense that changes in the lives of persons around us can have an impact on our own trajectories. Consider, for instance, how a 10-year-old daughter would be affected if her mother were convicted of a crime and sentenced to prison. In this case, an event in the mother's life would undoubtedly have a strong, and most likely negative, impact on the child's psychological and social development. The way in which we are linked to others influences who we are and who we become.

Even though families and other significant individuals help shape the life course, they represent only one source of influence on our lives. Broader social conditions and changes also influence the life course. Our lives carry the imprint of what happens in our particular social worlds. If our social world undergoes rapid change, it can disrupt our lives and change the timing and direction of important social events, such as marriage, having children, or pursuing an occupational career.

For example, during the Cultural Revolution in China in the late 1960s and early 1970s, the Chinese government implemented a policy of "sending-down" urban youths to live and work in rural areas. Being sent-down affected the youths' educational, family, and occupational trajectories. The longer the duration of the send-down experience, the more likely that marriage and childbearing would be delayed. For a generation of urban youth, the send-down policy radically changed the life course.

The Cultural Revolution and the send-down policy are dramatic examples of rapid social change. Wars and economic depressions are other examples. The Great Depression of the 1930s had profound effects on children raised during that period, and the nature of the effects varied, depending upon how old a child was when the depression began. Events such as the Cultural Revolution, the Great Depression, and world wars are the social equivalents of a large comet striking the earth. They shake things up dramatically, visibly, and quickly.

Other social changes occur incrementally and work their effects more slowly, less visibly, but just as profoundly nevertheless. Over the course of the past century and a half, American society has shifted from a farm-based rural society to a highly industrialized urban society. This change has taken place over several generations. Coinciding with the change from a rural to an urban society has been a change in the nature of work that has sharply altered the adolescent phase of the typical life course. Work has become less manual and more technical, requiring specialized skills, training, and education.

In the nineteenth century, by the time a young man reached the age of 16, he was more or less fully equipped to play a productive role in society and the economy. Most of the available work was farmrelated manual labor. It did not require special skills but rather strength, agility, and endurance, traits that teenagers and young adults have in abundance. Thus, young people between the ages of 16 and 20 were ready to assume adult roles in society. People tended to marry early and to start families early.

The transitions from child to adult to parent occurred over a shorter duration than they do now, and there was a closer connection between physical and social maturity. In the late twentieth and early twenty-first centuries in advanced societies, manual labor is becoming increasingly rare and increasingly poorly remunerated. Work requires technical skills and advanced education. As a result, young people are no longer able to assume productive roles in the adult economy. They must delay entry into the adult world of work and marriage in order to have time to pursue the education necessary to perform today's complex information-based work.

A gap has opened between the age at which people become physically mature and the age at which they become socially mature. This gap, sometimes called the maturity gap, represents a major change in the duration of the adolescent life stage and in the timing of important transitions. The widening of the maturity gap that has occurred throughout the twentieth century is an important factor in the rise and changing patterns of youth crime.

The life course perspective holds that human lives can be better understood if they are viewed in their changing worlds. We can call this the principle of contextualism, which holds that human development cannot be separated from the context in which it occurs. People cannot be separated from their time and place in history. Perhaps at no other time has the connection between biography and history been more telling than in the twentieth century.

Throughout the past century, monumental changes-two world wars, a profound economic depression, the rise and fall of communism, and technological advances in transportation and communication that were practically unimaginable at the beginning of the century-filled the historical record. All of these changes undoubtedly affected the lives of those who lived through them. Human development in the twentieth century cannot be understood in isolation from this ever-changing social environment.

To ignore social and historical change is to engage in a perverse and blinding form of tunnel vision. Related to the principle of contextualism is the life stage principle, which holds that the way that individual and social events affect life patterns is influenced by how old people are when events occur. The same event may have dramatically different effects, depending on the age of the person experiencing it. For example, a declaration of war will affect the lives of young children much differently than it will the lives of adult men.

As a criminological example of the life stage principle, consider how an arrest for illegal drug use may have different effects on the life course, depending on the age of the person who is arrested. If you were arrested at age 11 for such a crime, it would be a serious matter that probably would have profound consequences for your future life course. There is a good chance that you would be labeled a troublemaker and have difficulty completing school on time. Poor school performance, in turn, would reduce your future occupational opportunities. On the other hand, if you were able to avoid arrest until age 23, after you had a college degree in hand, the effects of this event would likely be less damaging.

Granted, being arrested at any age is not a good thing and is bound to reflect poorly on you. But in the years between ages 11 and 23 you would have had the opportunity to acquire human capital and presumably a track record of conforming behavior. You could call upon these assets to overcome the stigma and embarrassment of the arrest. Being arrested for the first time at age 11 is likely to be a life-changing event. Being arrested for the first time at age 23 is more likely to be an inconvenience. Thus, an arrest is an event in the life course. As with all events, its effects depend on the life stage at which it is experienced.

The fourth and final premise of the life course perspective follows from the other three. This premise is that efforts to optimize human development through preventive or corrective interventions will benefit if they are undertaken with sensitivity to the "particular age period in the framework of the entire life span". This premise simply alerts us that people are or can be influenced by different things at different stages of the life course, and it reflects another aspect of the life stage principle.

The timing of events and interventions is crucial to their effect. What may be an effective intervention strategy for an adult criminal may not work as well or at all for a troubled adolescent on the way toward becoming a juvenile delinquent. For example, recent research suggests that providing employment opportunities reduces recidivism among older criminals but has little effect on criminals in their teens or early twenties. Thus, the principle of timing relates to the effects of both unplanned events and planned interventions that occur in the life course.

Rise of Life Course Criminology

As with all theoretical developments in the social sciences, the life course approach to crime did not spring sui generis from the heads of contemporary criminologists. Rather, it evolved out of a theoretical context. This context is rooted most directly in the early twentieth century, when sociologists at the University of Chicago began conducting studies of problems confronting American society. These studies adopted what was essentially a life course perspective.

In The Polish Peasant in Europe and America, William I. Thomas and Florian Znaniecki used self-reported narratives of life histories from their subjects to trace patterns in experiences across generations. At approximately the same time, two longitudinal studies that focused on children born in the 1920s in California-the Oakland Growth Study and the Berkeley Guidance and Growth Studies-were initiated. These studies eventually collected data well into the 1980s and have been used to study variations in patterns of development and outcomes over a large segment of the life course.

American criminologists were not far behind sociologists in recognizing the potential insights that longitudinal studies might provide into their subject matter. By the 1930s, two important longitudinal studies of delinquents-the Crime Causation Study and the Cambridge-Somerville Youth Study-were underway.

In both stud-ies, data were collected on the subjects over the course of several decades. They serve as theoretical and empirical exemplars for contemporary longitudinal research on careers in crime. An important turning point in criminological research in the United States took place in Philadelphia in the 1960s, when a seminal birth cohort study was undertaken by MarvinWolfgang, Robert Figlio, and Thorsten Sellin. In this study, data were collected on a cohort of approximately 10,000 boys who were born in Philadelphia in 1945 and who lived there from the time they were 10 until they were at least 18. It is important because of the very detailed information it provided on the longitudinal sequencing of offenses in the cohort.

In 1986, the National Academy of Sciences published an influential two-volume report on career criminals and criminal careers. This report laid the groundwork for contemporary research on criminal careers and crime over the life course. The criminal career approach focuses on the activity of individuals who commit criminal offenses, and the criminal career is defined as the "longitudinal sequence of crimes committed by an individual offender". Criminal careers are characterized by four key dimensions. The dimension of participation distinguishes those who engage in crime at least once in their lifetimes from those who never engage in crime.

Current participation refers to those who engage in crime during a particular period in time from those who do not engage in crime during that period. The first time a person engages in crime, which is referred to as the age of onset, marks the beginning of a criminal career. Desistance is the term typically used to describe the end point of a criminal career. For life course researchers, age of onset is an important feature of the criminal career because it appears to be associated with the three other key dimensions of careers-frequency, seriousness, and career length. Frequency refers to an individual's rate of criminal activity, that is, to the number of offenses that the individual commits during a certain period of time. This rate is called lambda, λ.

Individual offending frequencies vary dramatically among offenders, with some having very high rates and others very low ones. Offending rates also may vary over time throughout an individual's criminal career.

Differences in λ are associated with demographic characteristics such as age, race, and sex, and with other factors, such as age of onset and drug use. Individuals who begin their criminal careers at younger ages generally have higher values for λ than those who begin later.

Active offenders who use drugs often commit offenses at relatively high rates. For life course researchers, an important question is what events or features of the life course influence individual offending rates. How does the life course of a high-rate offender differ from that of a low-rate offender? What factors are associated with increases or decreases in offending frequency?

Offenders also may vary in the seriousness of the offenses they commit. In regard to the dimension of seriousness, criminal career and life course researchers have invested considerable effort in trying to determine whether there are distinct types of criminal careers based on distinct patterns in offending seriousness. Do some offenders escalate in the seriousness of the offenses they commit as their careers progress, and if so, what factors distinguish those who escalate from those who do not? To what extent are minor and serious offenses randomly intermixed throughout the duration of the typical criminal career?

As offenders near the end of their criminal careers, do their offenses de-escalate in seriousness or do their offenses remain the same throughout their careers until desistance? Do individual offenders tend to specialize in particular types of offenses or are they generalists (that is, willing to engage in a wide variety of offense types)? These are some of the important questions criminal career and life course researchers continue to investigate.

Finally, researchers have focused closely on duration, or career length, as an important dimension of criminal careers. The research on duration consistently finds that criminal careers tend to be short, typically starting in the mid-teenage years and ending in the late teens or early 20s. But some individuals who initiate criminal careers as teenagers continue to commit offenses well into their 30s and beyond. Thus, it is important to understand the factors that distinguish offenders with long careers from those with short careers.

Likewise, life course researchers want to understand the relationship between duration and the other dimensions of criminal careers-frequency and seriousness. Do offenders with long careers tend to commit more serious offenses at higher rates than offenders with short careers, or are duration, frequency, and seriousness unrelated to one another?

What the life course perspective takes from the criminal career tradition is the idea that it is important to focus on the longitudinal sequencing of offenses and a recognition that the dimensions of criminal careers vary among individuals. What the life course perspective adds to the criminal career tradition is greater recognition of the reciprocal, mutually interacting connections between trajectories in crime and trajectories in other domains of life.

The life course perspective assumes that trajectories in crime represent only one limited part of individual life courses. It assumes that trajectories in crime can be better understood if they are viewed within the total context of the individual's life and development. Even the most serious high-rate repeat offenders engage in crime only for a relatively small part of each day.

The rest of the time they are doing other things. The life course perspective also is more attuned to the role of history and macrosociological factors in shaping criminal careers and individual life courses. Research on criminal careers has led to many important theoretical and policy-related findings in criminology. Nevertheless, like all research paradigms, it has its limitations. Because the life course perspective has been so closely connected to and shaped by the criminal career paradigm, it is imperative to be aware of those limitations.

One significant limitation involves the conceptualization of crime. In the United States, the vast majority of criminological research and theory focuses on ordinary street crime and on offenders who commit ordinary street crimes, that is, the index crimes that are tracked in the Federal Bureau of Investigation's annual Uniform Crime Report.

Our image of criminal careers and career criminals is based almost entirely on data collected from persons who have been arrested or incarcerated for index crimes. And it is probably fair to say that for most people the term "career criminal" brings to mind the image of an unrepentant, lifelong, "superpredator," as some commentators so vividly describe them. The stereotypical career criminal is a male who started offending early, commits serious crimes often, and spends much of his life incarcerated or running from the law.

By focusing so strongly on offenders who commit street crimes and on samples of persons who have been arrested or incarcerated, however, the career criminal approach ignores offenders who do not often appear in official statistics, such as those who commit white-collar crimes. It presents an image of criminal careers that is incomplete and based on class-biased samples of offenders and offenses. It may accurately describe the criminal careers of individuals who grow up in disadvantaged circumstances and who run afoul of the law early in life, but it tells us little or nothing about the criminal careers of individuals who commit white-collar crimes. Recent evidence suggests that careers in white-collar crime differ substantially from careers in street crime.

For now, we note that the life course perspective suffers from the same class-biased conceptualization of crime as the criminal career tradition. The factors that have been identified by life course researchers as important determinants of trajectories in street crime may not apply to those who commit white-collar crimes.

Trajectories and transitions: Recall that a trajectory is a sequence of linked states within a conceptually defined realm of behavior or experience. Trajectories are characterized by a number of dimensions that have consequences for how individuals develop. Three important dimensions are entrance, success, and timing. In regard to entrance, individuals can be described according to those trajectories they enter and those they do not. Not everyone has children; thus, not everyone has a parenthood trajectory.

Once individuals enter a particular trajectory, they can have varying levels of success in completing the typical tasks or activities that constitute that trajectory. For example, some people do well in school. At every level of their educational trajectories they stand out as overachievers. Others perform poorly. They may drop out of high school and never even get to college. Of special importance with respect to development over the life course is the matter of timing in trajectories. In every society, there are normatively defined correct times for individuals to enter or leave certain trajectories and to make transitions within trajectories.

In other words, trajectories are age graded. Transitions that are made at the right time are considered to be "age appropriate," whereas those that are made abnormally early or late are considered to be "off age". For example, in America it is age appropriate for children to leave their parental homes and to establish their own households sometime in their late teens or early 20s. Children who leave when they are much younger or who wait until they are in their 30s before leaving are making this transition at off-age times. Timing is important because transitions that are made off-age often have harmful consequences for other behavioral trajectories. For example, a child who leaves his or her parental home at a young age is at great risk of failing to complete schooling and may end up homeless and living on the street.

Transitions also are important because they can represent turning points or change in the life course. For example, a juvenile delinquent who finds a good job as he enters adulthood and who desists from crime as a result of having stable employment has undergone an important turning point in the life course. His trajectory in crime exhibits change in behavior. On the other hand, some delinquents do not desist from crime as they enter adulthood. Their crime trajectories are characterized by continuity throughout the life course. A trademark of life course studies is the dual focus on continuity and change. Life course researchers attempt to understand how childhood or adolescent experiences are linked to adult outcomes and how transitions or turning points may lead to change in life course trajectories.

Cumulative continuity and self-selection: A particularly important issue in the life course perspective involves the distinction between cumulative continuity and self-selection. Cumulative continuity refers to the way in which behavior at one point in life influences opportunities and behavior later in life. For example, a young boy who is arrested early in life may be labeled a troublemaker by the police, teachers, and other adults. Because he has been labeled a troublemaker, the boy may be prevented from associating with the "good" kids in his neighborhood and forced to find companionship with other known troublemakers.

Hanging around with other troublemakers leads naturally to more trouble and more run-ins with the police. In this case, the boy's early arrest leads to subsequent arrests and eventually to the accumulation of an extensive criminal record. Another example of cumulative continuity might involve doing poorly in high school, which closes off educational and occupational opportunities, leading to unemployment later in life. In regard to crime, cumulative continuity refers to a dynamic process in which delinquent behavior at one point in time has consequences that increase the likelihood of continued delinquent behavior at later points in time.

For example, two well-known life course researchers, Robert J. Sampson and John Laub, argue that the most important consequence of delinquent behavior is that it may block the individual's opportunity to develop adult social bonds. Serious delinquency may lead to a "knifing off" of future opportunities. The process of cumulative continuity leads eventually to cumulative disadvantage, a piling up of negative experiences and failures that make it difficult for a person to succeed in life.

Cumulative continuity is different from self-selection: Self-selection refers to the tendency of individuals to select experiences that are consistent with internal traits or dispositions that are established early in life. For example, an antisocial child becomes an antisocial adult whose antisocial nature leads to marital and occupational instability as well as unsuccessful performance in other life domains. Statistically, self-selection means that correlations between adult crime and other adult behaviors are spurious and will disappear if controls for prior individual-level differences in internal traits are used. Statistically, self-selection also means that the correlation between delinquent behavior at one point in time and delinquent behavior at a later point in time is spurious or not causal.

Both early and late offenses are caused by the internal traits of the individual. Early offenses do not independently increase the likelihood of later offenses through the process of cumulative continuity. The distinction between self-selection and cumulative continuity is the same as the distinction between state dependence and population heterogeneity. If participation in delinquency at Time 1 has a behavioral impact on the future conduct of the individual, that is state dependence. State dependence could explain the well-known positive correlation between past and future delinquency.

On the other hand, population heterogeneity might also account for the association. Population heterogeneity refers to an unmeasured propensity toward delinquency over time. People high in this propensity will commit crimes at every stage of the life course, whereas people low in propensity will not commit crime. Over time, crime or delinquency at Time 1 will be positively correlated with crime or delinquency at Time 2.

Ontogenesis and the ontogenetic fallacy: Because the life course perspective incorporates the biological dimension, it is important to understand the terms ontogenesis and ontogenetic fallacy. Ontogenesis refers to the origin and development of an individual and to the way in which personal biologically based traits influence this process. The ontogenetic fallacy is the "fallacy of attributing developmental outcomes solely to the unfolding of personal traits and ignoring that it is the interaction between traits and the environment that produces the outcome" .

For example, to say that a person succeeded in college solely because he or she was born with a high IQ is to commit the ontogenetic fallacy, because in reality this outcome-academic success-results from the interaction of the person's IQ with a host of other factors, such as his or her social class origins and parents' wishes.

Cohorts and age: A cohort is defined as a group of individuals who experience the "same event within the same time interval". Typically, the defining event is birth. For example, in the Philadelphia study, Wolfgang, Figlio, and Sellin studied a birth cohort whose members were all boys born in 1945. Although cohorts are most often defined by age, the sharing of some other common characteristic can identify them. For example, a cohort may be defined in terms of year of marriage or year of entering college. Life course researchers depend heavily on longitudinal studies that are designed to gather data on cohorts of individuals that are followed over time.

Recent cohort studies have been based on cohorts defined by relatively narrow age ranges of between one to three years, but sometimes larger age ranges are used. Different age cohorts may be compared with one another to observe what are known as cohort effects. A cohort effect is said to be present when members of different cohorts vary significantly in some characteristic. For example, a cohort effect appeared to be present when the 1945 Philadelphia cohort was compared to a cohort of Philadelphia children born in 1958.

The 1958 cohort had much higher levels of violent crime when they were teenagers than the 1945 cohort did at the same age. A cohort effect might also arise if cohorts respond differently to an historical event. For example, the impact of a dramatic event such as a war or a depression may affect individuals differently, depending on their age when the event occurred. War has a different meaning and is a different experience for a 10-year-old boy than it is for a 20-year-old young man. This difference is a cohort effect. Cohort effects are important for the life course perspective, because they signal the likely presence of macrohistorical influences on the structure of the life course.

Bound up with the concepts of cohort and cohort effect are the twin concepts of social age and historical age. Social age refers to the norms and expectations that impinge upon people at different ages. There are normatively defined "right" times to experience or accomplish major events and transitions, such as getting married, having children, getting a job, and finishing school. Making a transition out of sequence or at an unusual time has normative and demographic consequences.

Historical age relates to one's cohort. Age may have different meanings, depending on cohort or historical position. Being 16 in 1998 is different from being 16 in 1898. Historical age and social age are connected in that the meaning or implications of events and transitions may vary depending on when they are experienced historically. Elder gives the example of young children experiencing divorce during periods of low versus rapidly rising divorce rates. Divorce is likely to be a more traumatizing and stigmatizing event for a child during periods when it is uncommon than in periods when many of the child's friends have divorced parents. The meaning of social age thus may change over historical periods, which would influence the impact of events on life patterns.

Research designs: The life course perspective assumes that events that happen at one time in life affect events at later times. The concept of trajectory implies momentum and continuity in behavior, psychological functioning, and biological development over time. Methodological consequences follow from these theoretical assumptions. The most important of these consequences is that life course research must be carried out using longitudinal research designs.

Hence, it is important to understand the features and types of longitudinal research designs. There are two basic types of longitudinal research designs that have often been used in life course research: prospective and retrospective. Each has strengths and weaknesses. Prospective designs follow a sample, usually a cohort of similarly aged individuals, over time.

At the start of the study, baseline data is collected on the sample subjects. At periodic intervals thereafter, the researchers collect new data on the subjects. Thus, for example, a sample of children aged 10 may be selected and followed for a 10-year period until they reach age 20, with data collected every two years. In criminological life course research, data typically come from interviews with the subjects, but data may also be collected from parents and teachers as well as from official records of schools and law enforcement agencies.

The primary advantage of prospective designs is that information on events can be collected relatively soon after they happen, before they have been distorted by the subject's retrospective reinterpretation. A boy interviewed at age 16 would probably be able to provide a more accurate self-report of his criminal activity at age 15 than he would if the interview was delayed until he reached age 25. The disadvantage of prospective studies for criminological research is that they may be uneconomical for serious crimes, depending on how the sample is drawn.

Samples may be drawn from the general population, and these are known as normal or population samples; alternatively, samples may be drawn from high-risk or clinical populations. Because prospective studies generally start with samples of relatively young children, it is not known in advance how many of the sample subjects will engage in serious crimes during the course of the study. The prevalence of serious index-type crimes, such as murder, robbery, rape, and aggravated assault, is relatively low in the general population.

If researchers simply draw a random sample of, say, 400 children, they may find that none or only a very few of the children will engage in serious crimes over the course of the study. The small number of serious offenders reduces statistical power and makes it more difficult for researchers to draw conclusions about the factors that distinguish serious from nonserious offenders. One way around this problem is to draw large samples, but that is expensive. The other solution is to draw what are known as high-risk samples, that is, samples in which the subjects come from social backgrounds that tend to have higher rates of criminal offending than normal.

For example, rather than taking a random sample of children in a school system, researchers may restrict their sample to children who reside in disadvantaged neighborhoods, where crime is common. This strategy increases the likelihood that a sufficiently large number of individuals who will engage in serious crime will be included in the sample.

Both normal and high-risk sampling designs may be combined in a single study. Researchers may, for example, take a random sample of the general population and then another sample of similar size from a high-risk population. Through the use of statistical weighting procedures the two samples may be combined. In a retrospective longitudinal design, the sample subjects are typically older and are selected because they meet some criteria established by the study. After the sample is selected, the researchers gather data from various sources on the subjects' past experiences.

For example, researchers might select a sample of adult prison inmates and interview them about their family backgrounds and criminal activities when they were younger. The obvious disadvantages of retrospective interviews are the problems of forgetfulness and reinterpretation of events. As time passes, most of us forget things, and we have a tendency to distort or selectively reinterpret past events in order to make sense of our present situation. Researchers using retrospective designs try to correct for these problems by using a special interviewing technique known as a life history calendar.

A life history calendar is a large grid-shaped chart. On the left side of the grid are listed details of behavioral patterns that are being investigated, such as types of crimes. The top side is divided into time units for which behavior patterns can be recorded. For example, a life history calendar might be constructed to gather data on the timing of delinquent acts by a juvenile and events in his or her family life.

The life history calendar helps improve the quality of retrospective data because it permits the respondent to relate the timing of events both visually and mentally. Researchers may also supplement interviews by checking official records to reconstruct the subjects' trajectories in crime. But official records have their shortcomings, too. They only include acts that come to the attention of authorities. Furthermore, official records are compiled to meet the needs of bureaucracies, not researchers. They often do not contain information on concepts and issues relevant to researchers.

For criminological research, the main advantage of retrospective designs is that they permit researchers to draw samples that meet the needs of their research questions. For example, they can draw samples that include adequate numbers of serious offenders for statistical analysis.

Developmental Studies

These studies have served as the basis for literally hundreds, if not thousands, of publications on issues related to crime and the life course. In some cases, the original collectors of the data have made them available for use by other researchers. To help familiarize you with the methodological details of the major studies in life course criminology. The studies are presented roughly in the chronological order of when data collection was initiated.

Deviant Children Grown Up: This famous study was conducted by Lee Robins and Patricia O'Neal. It attempted to describe the natural histories of subjects who displayed antisocial personalities and behavior. Data collection began in 1924. It is a complex study that involves three different cohorts. The first cohort included 524 white subjects under the age of 18, selected from the patients of a municipal child-guidance clinic in St. Louis, Missouri.

The second cohort was designed to serve as a control for the first. It included 100 white elementary-school students of the same-age and sex distribution as the first cohort and from the same census tracts. For cohorts 1 and 2, data were collected in two waves. Wave 1 lasted from 1924 to 1929, and wave 2 lasted from 1955 to 1960. In the second wave, the subjects ranged in age from 30 to 55. The third cohort consisted of the sons of cohorts 1 and 2 (N = 67). Data were collected from a variety of sources, including personal interviews, official police and court records, school records, and mental health agency records.

Cambridge-Somerville Youth Study: The Cambridge-Somerville Youth Study was the brainchild of Dr. Richard Clarke Cabot, a physician and social philosopher who believed that delinquency could be prevented if potential delinquents had an opportunity to form a strong bond with an understand-ing adult early in life. Beginning in 1937, Dr. Cabot initiated a study that eventually involved 650 high-risk and low-risk boys from disadvantaged neighborhoods in Cambridge, Massachusetts. Boys randomly selected from high-risk and low-risk pools were paired by age, background, and personality. Half the boys were placed in a treatment group and half in a control group.

The treatment group was supposed to receive treatment in the form of a close, intimate friendship with a counselor, but in most cases the treatment did not achieve this ideal. The idea was to determine whether the treated boys fared better than the control group in avoiding delinquency. The sample was 95 percent white and mostly from poor or working-class backgrounds. Sample ages ranged from 4 to 11 at the start of study. A full range of data was collected on life history variables and criminal history. Three waves of data were collected in 1936-37, 1939-45, and 1975-76. In the final wave, subjects were between the ages of 43 and 50.

Crime Causation Study

Unraveling Juvenile Delinquency: Sheldon and Eleanor Glueck were pioneers in the use of longitudinal research designs in criminology. During their long tenure at Harvard University, they conducted several longitudinal studies of delinquents and nondelinquents in Massachusetts. Their most wellknown investigation, the Crime Causation Study: Unraveling Juvenile Delinquency (UJD), was the basis for several books. This study began in 1939 with a sample of 1,000 boys aged 10 to 17 from disadvantaged neighborhoods in Boston. A unique feature of the UJD study was its matching design.

Half of the sample, 500 boys, were officially defined delinquents, selected from the rosters of two facilities for juvenile delinquents in Boston. The other half of the sample consisted of 500 nondelinquent boys who were matched with the delinquents on age, race and ethnicity, and intelligence. All of the boys were white. Between 1939 and 1948, detailed information on the delinquents and nondelinquents was collected. The data covered social, psychological, and biological characteristics, family life, school perfor-mance, work experience, delinquent behavior, and other life events.

A great strength of the Gluecks' datacollection procedures was the use of multiple respondents and multiple data sources. Information about the boys and their families was gathered through interviews with the boys themselves and with their parents, teachers, neighbors, and criminal justice officials. Measures of delinquency came from self-reports, parent reports, and teacher reports and were supplemented with checks of official records. Between 1949 and 1963, the Gluecks conducted follow-ups on the original sample at age 25 and again at age 32.

Thus, data are available from childhood through young adulthood. The retention rate for the follow-ups was extraordinarily good. Sampson and Laub calculate that the follow-up success rate is approximately 92 percent, adjusted for mortality. Data from all three age periods are available for 438 of the 500 delinquents and 442 of the nondelinquent controls. After lying dormant in Harvard Law School Library for nearly two decades, the UJD data were rediscovered by Robert Sampson and John Laub.

They undertook to recode and computerize the original paper case files, an exceedingly complicated and daunting task. After several years, they succeeded in reconstructing the data and eventually used them as the major source of information for their book Crime in the Making: Pathways and Turning Points Through Life, arguably the most important work yet published on crime from the life course perspective.

PHILADELPHIA COHORT STUDIES

There are two Philadelphia cohort studies. The first, and most famous, of the pair of studies followed an unselected cohort of 9,945 boys who were born in 1945 and who resided in Philadelphia between their 10th and 18th birthdays. The researchers collected data on the boys from official police records and from schools and other governmental agencies. In the original study, interviews were not conducted with the members of the cohort. However, in a later extension of the study, interviews were conducted with a 10 percent random sample of the original cohort, approximately 975 men.

The interviews took place when the subjects were age 26 and collected detailed information on their marital, educational, and occupational histories, as well as information on criminal behavior and victimization experiences. The second of the Philadelphia studies followed a larger cohort of over 27,000 individuals born in Philadelphia in 1958. Girls were included in this cohort. Data were collected from police and district attorney records, personal interviews, and self-enumerated questionnaires.

The sample was followed up to 1988, when they were 30 years of age. Information is available on offenses committed while the members of the cohort were juveniles and while they were adults. Designed and conducted by Lyle Shannon, this study contains data on juvenile delinquency and adult crime for three birth cohorts born in 1942, 1949, and 1955 in Racine, Wisconsin. Shannon used personal interviews and police and court records to gather data on the cohorts. The sample sizes for 1942, 1949, and 1955 are 1,352, 2,099, and 2,676, respectively. A unique feature of this study is the availability of ecological data on the neighborhoods in which the members of each cohort resided in Racine. Shannon supplemented the individual-level data with census data for each city block in Racine for 1950, 1960, and 1970. In addition, other ecological data were gathered from land-use maps and city directories.

Delinquent Development Study

The Cambridge Study in Delinquent Development is an important long-term prospective study of crime and delinquency among 411 inner-city males who were born around 1953. At the time they were selected for inclusion in the study, all were living in a workingclass area of London. The study was originally directed by Donald J. West and is now under the direction of David P. Farrington. Analyses of data collected during this study have resulted in four books and over 60 articles. Throughout the Cambridge study, data have been collected from multiple sources, including the subjects, their parents, teachers, peers, and official sources.

As of 1990, eight personal interviews had been conducted with the subjects from age 8 to age 32. The attrition rate for the study has been very low. Up through age 32, the researchers have been able to keep in touch with 94 percent of the original sample. Information has been collected on a very wide array of theoretical dimensions, such as intelligence, personality, parent-child relationship, delinquency of peers, school performance, marital stability, and employment histories.

Understanding and Prediction of Delinquent Child Behavior: This study is based on a relatively small sample of 206 males in Eugene, Oregon. Data collection began in 1984, when males from high-risk, fourth-grade classrooms were selected. At the start of the study, subjects were 9 to 11 years old. Most of the subjects are white and from poor or working-class families. Data were collected annually from 1984 to 1989. The distinguishing feature of this study is the detailed collection of measures of family processes. The researchers have constructed a theory of family processes as they relate to delinquency that has been highly influential in the life course perspective.

Program of Research on the Causes and Correlates of Delinquency: The Causes and Correlates of Delinquency Program encompasses three federally funded longitudinal research projects located in three cities-Denver, Colorado, Pittsburgh, Pennsylvania, and Rochester, New York. The program was initiated in 1986 by the U.S. Department of Justice's Office of Juvenile Justice and Delinquency Prevention. Different teams of researchers conduct the projects at the three sites, but there is extensive communication and coordination of research activities among the research teams.

All the projects use a similar research design that consists of a longitudinal investigation of high-risk inner-city youth during their developmental years. In each project, the researchers have conducted regular face-to-face interviews with the research subjects. The interviews with the youths are supplemented by interviews with parents or other caretakers and with teachers. Official data from police, courts, schools, and social service agencies on each subject are also collected. A unique feature of the Causes and Correlates of Delinquency Program is the use of common measures of important concepts such as self-reported delinquency, drug use, community and neighborhood characteristics, a host of youth, family, and peer variables, and arrest and judicial-processing histories.

At all three sites, researchers have maintained high sample retention rates. The Denver Youth Survey sample includes 806 boys and 721 girls who were selected from randomly chosen households in disadvantaged neighborhoods. Data collection began in 1987, when the children were 7, 9, 11, 13, or 15 years old. Between 1988 and 1992, the youths and their caretakers were interviewed annually. Annual interviews were also conducted from 1995 up to 1999. The Pittsburgh Youth Study sample was assembled in stages. First, the researchers selected and screened a random sample of boys in the first, fourth, and seventh grades of the Pittsburgh public school system.

Based on the initial screening, the researchers identified the 30 percent of boys with the most disruptive behavior. These boys were included in the final study sample along with a random sample of the remaining 70 percent of boys. This procedure resulted in a total sample of 1,517 boys, with approximately 500 coming from each grade level. Subjects and their caretakers were interviewed at six-month intervals for the first five years of the study. Teachers were also asked to rate the subjects. After seven assessments, the researchers stopped collecting data on the middle sample (fourth grade).

Interviews with the two other samples have continued on an annual basis. The Rochester Youth Development Study involves 1,000 students randomly selected from students in the seventh and eighth grades of the Rochester public schools in spring 1988. Subjects and their caretakers were interviewed at six-month intervals from 1988 to 1992 and annually from 1994 to 1996.

National Youth Survey (NYS)

The National Youth Survey (NYS) began in 1976. It is a prospective longitudinal study of a representative sample of 1,725 youths aged 11 to 17 at the start of the study. Thus, it includes seven birth cohorts. As of 1994, nine waves of data had been collected. Interviews with the sample subjects are supplemented with official record data. Official record data are also available for the parents or primary caretakers of the subjects.

The NYS was designed to provide a "comprehensive description of the prevalence and incidence of delinquent behavior and drug use in the American youth population". It contains extensive and detailed measures of concepts drawn from strain and control theories, and has been used to construct and evaluate an integrated theoretical model of delinquent behavior. A great strength of the NYS is that it is based on a national probability sample of American youth. Hence, results based on the NYS can be generalized to the population of American youth. Many other longitudinal studies are based on samples drawn from high-risk populations, making it difficult to use them to draw firm conclusions about youth in general.

Multidisciplinary Health and Development Study

The Multidisciplinary Health and Development Study is set in Dunedin, New Zealand. It is a prospective longitudinal cohort study of an unselected population. The cohort consists of all children born at the only maternity hospital in Dunedin between April 1, 1972, and March 31, 1973, who were still living in the local province when the study began three years later, in 1975. At that time, 1,139 of the children were eligible for the study and 1,037 participated. The sample has been assessed every two years since 1975 with an extensive array of psychological, medical, and sociological measures. Interviews are conducted with the subjects, their parents, and their teachers. Official record data also are collected.

Human Development: PHDCN Project

The Project on Human Development in Chicago Neighborhoods (PHDCN) is a mammoth research effort jointly funded by the National Institute of Justice, National Institute of Mental Health, U.S. Department of Education, and the John D. and Catherine T. MacArthur Foundation. There are two major parts to the study. One part of the study, which focuses on Chicago's neighborhoods, is divided into three components.

The first component of the neighborhood study includes in-person interviews with a randomly selected sample of more than 8,700 residents of all Chicago neighborhoods. The interviews covered a variety of community-related issues, such as perceived violence and neighborhood decline. For the second component of the neighborhood study, 80 neighborhoods were selected for systematic social observation. Researchers videotape blocks in the 80 neighborhoods to record "life and behavior in each neighborhood".

The final component of the neighborhood study is a survey of neighborhood leaders and experts. For life course researchers, the second part of the study may be more interesting than the community study. The second part of the PHDCN is a longitudinal cohort study of 7,000 individuals ranging in age from birth to 18. The cohort sample will be drawn from the 80 neighborhoods undergoing systematic social observation. In the cohort study, equal numbers of males and females in seven age cohorts (birth, 3, 6, 9, 12, 15, 18) are being selected from African-American, Hispanic, white, and mixed-ethnic communities.

All social classes are included. Each cohort will be assessed annually for eight years via interviews with the subjects (for those old enough) and their caretakers. Because it includes data on both individuals and communities, the PHDCN is potentially an extremely important study. Researchers will be able to investigate in more detail than ever before possible the links between individuals, families, and communities in shaping developmental trajectories. Several articles have been published from the community design phase of the study. No results have yet been published from the cohort study.

U.S. government agencies support a number of longitudinal studies of different segments of the U.S. population. Some of these studies include subjects and measures useful for life course research on criminological issues. Two important studies that have been used for criminological research are the National Longitudinal Survey of Labor Market Experiences and the National Longitudinal Survey of Youth. The main advantage of these studies is that they are based on large unselected or normal samples of the population.

Thus, unlike some criminological research projects that rely on high-risk samples, these studies permit researchers to investigate criminological and life course issues in samples with a broad range of variation in class-linked variables. A weakness of these studies for criminological research is that the measures of criminality are often not detailed. In addition, data usually are collected only from the sample subjects. Other persons related to the subjects, such as parents and teachers, are not contacted. As a result, measurement error and data validity are more problematic.

5

Sampling

Sampling is the procedure a researcher uses to gather people, places, or things to study. Research conclusions and generalizations are only as good as the sample they are based on. Samples are always subsets or small parts of the total number that could be studied. If you were to sample everybody and everything, that would be called a quota sample.

Most research, however, involves non-quota samples. For example, if you were interested in state prison systems, you might sample 15 or so state prison systems. There are formulas for determining sample size, but the main thing is to be practical. For a small population of interest, you would most likely need to sample about 10-30% of that population; for a large population of interest (over 150,000), you could get by with a sample as low as 1%.

Before gathering your sample, it's important to find out as much as possible about your population. Population refers to the larger group from which the sample is taken. You should at least know some of the overall demographics; age, sex, class, etc., about your population. This information will be needed later after you get to the data analysis part of your research, but it's also important in helping you decide sample size. The greater the diversity and differences that exist in your population, the larger your sample size should be.

Capturing the variability in your population allows for more variation in your sample, and since many statistical tests operate on the principles of variation, you'll be making sure the statistics used later can do their powerful stuff. After you've learned all the theoretically important things about your population, you then have to obtain a list or contact information on those who are accessible or can be contacted. This procedure for listing all the accessible members of your population is called the sampling frame.

If you were planning on doing a phone survey, for example, the phone book would be your sampling frame. Make sure your sampling frame is appropriate for the population you want to study. In this case, the Census Dept. says that 93% of us have a phone, so that's not too bad, but you have to decide if any of the unique characteristics of people you're interested in studying are lost by selecting a restrictive sampling frame. The term refers to the procedure rather than the list. It's important for researchers to discuss their sampling frame because that's what ensures that systematic error.

There are two basic approaches to sampling: probabilistic and nonprobabilistic. If the purpose of your research is to draw conclusions or make predictions affecting the population as a whole (as most research usually is), then you must a use probabilistic sampling approach. On the other hand, if you're only interested in seeing how a small group, perhaps even a representative group, is doing for purposes of illustration or explanation, then you can use a nonprobabilistic sampling approach.

The key component behind all probabilistic sampling approaches is randomization, or random selection. Don't confuse random selection with random assignment. Random selection is how you draw the sample. Random assignment is how you assign people in your sample to different groups for experimental or control group purposes. People, places, or things are randomly selected when each unit in the population has an equal chance of being selected. Various methods have been established to accomplish probabilistic sampling:

— *Simple random sampling*: All you need is a relatively small, self-contained, or clearly defined population to use this method. The population of the U.S. might be too big, but a city of say 60,000 or so would be appropriate. You simply obtain a list of all residents, and then using a sequence of numbers from a random numbers table (or draws of a hat, flips of a coin), select, say 10%, 20%, or some portion of names on that list, making sure you aren't drawing from any letter of the alphabet more heavily than others.

— *Stratified random sampling*: This method is appropriate when you're interested in correcting for gender, race, or age disparities in your population. Say you're planning to study the impact of police training on mid-level career cynicism, and you know that gender is going to be an important factor because female police officers rarely take this kind of training and/or quit before making it to their mid-level career stage.

You therefore need to stratify your sample by the gender strata, making sure that you oversample females (draw more of random number of females) as opposed to males. For example, if the department has 1000 employees consisting of 900 males and 100 females, and you intend on sampling 10% of the total, then you proceed randomly as usual, drawing 90 males at random and 10 females at random. If you had used the employee list of names, regardless of gender, you might not have obtained 10 females at random because there's so few of them.

— *Systematic random sampling:* Suppose you had a huge list of people, places, or things to select from, like

100,000 people or more. The appropriate method to use is to select every 10th, 20th, or 30th person from that list. Your decision to use every 10th, 20th, or 30th person is called your sampling interval, and as long as you do it systematically and use the entire list, you're accomplishing the same thing as random sampling.

— *Cluster (area) random sampling*: Suppose you have a population that is dispersed across a wide geographic region. This method allows you to divide this population into clusters (usually counties, census tracts, or other boundaries) and then randomly sample everyone in those clusters. For example, you could randomly select 5 of North Carolina's 100 counties, but you would have to make sure that almost every person in those 5 counties participated in your study. As an alternative, you could systematically sample within your clusters, and this is called multi-stage sampling, which refers generally to any mixing of sampling methods.

Various methods have also been established to accomplish nonprobabilistic sampling:

— *Quota sampling*: As discussed earlier, sampling everybody and everything is quota sampling. The problem with it is that bias intrudes on the sampling frame. One the researcher identifies the people to be studied, they have to resort to haphazard or accidental sampling because no effort is usually made to contact people who are difficult to reach in the quota.

— *Convenience sampling*: Also called haphazard or accidental, this method is based on using people who are a captive audience, just happen to be walking by, or show a special interest in your research. The use of volunteers is an example of convenience sampling.

— *Purposive sampling*: This is where the researcher targets a group of people believed to be typical or average, or a group of people specially picked for some unique purpose. The researcher never knows if the sample is representative of the population, and this method is largely limited to exploratory research.

— *Snowball sampling* : Also called network, chain, or reputational, this method begins with a few people or cases and then gradually increases the sample size as new contacts are mentioned by the people you started out with.

Sampling Distribution

The sampling distribution is a hypothetical device that figuratively represents the distribution of a statistic (some number you've obtained from your sample) across an infinite number of samples. You have to remember than your sample is just one of a potentially infinite number of samples that could have been drawn.

While it's very likely that any statistics you generate from your sample would be near the center of the sampling distribution, just by luck of the draw, the researcher normally wants to find out exactly where the center of this sampling distribution is. That's because the center of the sampling distribution represents the best estimate of the population average, and the population is what you want to make inferences to.

The average of the sampling distribution is the population parameter, and inference is all about making generalizations from statistics (sample) to parameters (population). You can use some of the information you've collected thus far to calculate the sampling distribution, or more accurately, the sampling error. In statistics, any standard deviation of a sampling distribution is referred to as the standard error (to keep it separate in our minds from standard deviation). In sampling, the standard error is referred to as sampling error. Definitions are as follows:

— *Standard deviation*: the spread of scores around the average in a single sample

— *Standard error*: the spread of averages around the average of averages in a hypothetical sampling distribution

You never actually see the sampling distribution. All you have to work with is the standard deviation of your sample. The greater your standard deviation, the greater the standard error (and your sampling error). Standard error is also related to sample size. The larger your sample, the smaller the standard error.

You're not reducing bias or anything by increasing sample size, only coming closer to the total number in the population. Validity and sampling error are somewhat similar. However, you can estimate population parameters from even small samples.

The best way to estimate population parameters is to use a confidence interval approach. Take the mean score on some variable in your sample and calculate the standard deviation for it. Then, assuming a bell-shaped curve, add your standard deviation to the mean (going one direction on the x-axis under the curve), and then subtract your standard deviation from the mean (going the other direction).

The standard rule is that 65% of cases in real life (the population) will be between these extremes. If you add and substract two standard deviations from the mean, another rule states that approximately 95% of scores in real life will fall between these two extremes. All you need to know is how to calculate a standard deviation, and the formula appears below:

$$\sqrt{\frac{\Sigma(X-\overline{X})^2}{(n-1)}}$$

Where

X = each score

$\overline{X}$ = the mean or average

n = the number of values

S means we sum acroos the values

If you go out three standard deviations, you include 99% of the cases. With the 65, 95, and 99 percent rules, you are actually predicting population characteristics, and all this from just your sample. You've made the first application of your research study to the wider population of interest.

6

Levels of Measurement

Measurement is the assignment of numbers to things. Measurement is at the core of doing research. In almost all research, everything has to be reduced to numbers eventually. Precision and exactness in measurement are vitally important. The measures are what are actually used to test the hypotheses. A researcher needs good measures for both independent and dependent variables.

Measurement consists of two basic processes called conceptualization and operationalization, then an advanced process called determining the levels of measurement, and then even more advanced methods of measuring reliability and validity. Conceptualization is the process of taking a construct or concept and refining it by giving it a conceptual or theoretical definition. Ordinary dictionary definitions will not do. Instead, the researcher takes keywords in their research question or hypothesis and finds a clear and consistent definition that is agreed-upon by others in the scientific community.

Sometimes, the researcher pushes the envelope by coming up with a novel conceptual definition, but such initiatives are rare and require the researcher to have intimate familiarity with the topic. More common is the process by which a researcher notes agreements and disagreements over conceptualization in the literature review, and then comes down in favor of someone else's conceptual definition. It's perfectly acceptable in science to borrow the conceptualizations and operationalizations of others.

Conceptualization is often guided by the theoretical framework, perspective, or approach the researcher is committed to. For example, a researcher operating from within a Marxist framework would have quite different conceptual definitions for a hypothesis about social class and crime than a non-Marxist researcher. That's because there are strong value positions in different theoretical perspectives about how some things should be measured. Most criminal justice researchers at this point will at least decide what type of crime they're going to study.

Operationalization is the process of taking a conceptual definition and making it more precise by linking it to one or more specific, concrete indicators or operational definitions. These are usually things with numbers in them that reflect empirical or observable reality. For example, if the type of crime one has chosen to study is theft (as representative of crime in general), creating an operational definition for it means at least choosing between petty theft and grand theft.

Some researchers do, but most often, operational definitions are also borrowed or created anew. They're what link the world of ideas to the world of everyday reality. It's more important that ordinary people would agree on your indicators than other scientists or legislators, but again, avoid dictionary definitions. If you were to use legalistic definitions, then it's your duty to provide what is called an auxiliary theory, which is a justification for the research utility of legal hair-splitting.

The most important thing to remember at this point, however, is your unit of analysis. You want to make absolutely sure that everything you reduce down is defined at the same unit of analysis: societal, regional, state, communal, individual, to name a few. You don't want to end up with a research project that has to collect political science data, sociological data, and psychological data. In most cases, you should break it all down so that each variable is operationally defined at the same level of thought, attitude, trait, or behavior, although some would call this psychological reductionism and are more comfortable with group-level units or psychological units only as a proxy measure for more abstract, harder-to-measure terms.

A level of measurement is the precision by which a variable is measured. For 50 years, with few detractors, science has used the Stevens typology of measurement levels. There are three things to remember about this typology:

- anything that can be measured falls into one of the four types;
- the higher the type, the more precision in measurement; and
- every level up contains all the properties of the previous level.

The four levels of measurement, from lowest to highest, are:

- Nominal
- Ordinal
- Interval
- Ratio

The nominal level of measurement describes variables that are categorical in nature. The characteristics of the data you're collecting fall into distinct categories. If there are a limited number of distinct categories (usually only two), then you're dealing with a discrete variable. If there are an unlimited or infinite number of distinct categories, then you're dealing with a continuous variable. Nominal variables include demographic characteristics like sex, race, and religion.

The ordinal level of measurement describes variables that can be ordered or ranked in some order of importance. It describes most judgments about things, such as big or little, strong or weak. Most opinion and attitude scales or indexes in the social sciences are ordinal in nature. The interval level of measurement describes variables that have more or less equal intervals, or meaningful distances between their ranks. For example, if you were to ask somebody if they were first, second, or third generation immigrant, the assumption is that the distance, or number of years, between each generation is the same.

All crime rates in criminal justice are interval level measures, as is any kind of rate. The ratio level of measurement describes variables that have equal intervals and a fixed zero (or reference) point. It is possible to have zero income, zero education, and no involvement in crime, but rarely do we see ratio level variables in social science since it's almost impossible to have zero attitudes on things, although "not at all", "often", and "twice as often" might qualify as ratio level measurement.

Advanced statistics require at least interval level measurement, so the researcher always strives for this level, accepting ordinal level (which is the most common) only when they have to. Variables should be conceptually and operationally defined with levels of measurement in mind since it's going to affect how well you can analyze your data later on.

Reliability and Validity

For a research study to be accurate, its findings must be reliable and valid. Reliability means that the findings would be consistently the same if the study were done over again. It sounds easy, but think of a typical exam in college; if you scored a 74 on that exam, don't you think you would score differently if you took if over again? Validity refers to the truthfulness of findings; if you really measured what you think you measured, or more precisely, what others think you measured.

Again, think of a typical multiple choice exam in college; does it really measure proficiency over the subject matter, or is it really measuring IQ, age, test-taking skill, or study habits?. A study can be reliable but not valid, and it cannot be valid without first being reliable. You cannot assume validity no matter how reliable your measurements are. There are many different threats to validity as well as reliability, but an important early consideration is to ensure you have internal validity.

This means that you are using the most appropriate research design for what you're studying (experimental, quasi-experimental, survey, qualitative, or historical), and it also means that you have screened out spurious variables as well as thought out the possible contamination of other variables creeping into your study. Anything you do to standardize or clarify your measurement instrument to reduce user error will add to your reliability.

It's also important early on to consider the time frame that is appropriate for what you're studying. Some social and psychological phenomena (most notably those involving behavior or action) lend themselves to a snapshot in time. If so, your research need only be carried out for a short period of time, perhaps a few weeks or a couple of months.

In such a case, your time frame is referred to as cross-sectional. Sometimes, cross-sectional research is criticized as being unable to determine cause and effect, and a longer time frame is called for, one that is called longitudinal, which may add years onto carrying out your research. There are many different types of longitudinal research, such as those that involve tracking a cohort of subjects (such as schoolchildren across grade levels), or those that involve time-series (such as tracking a third world nation's economic development over four years or so). The general rule is to use longitudinal research the greater the number of variables you've got operating in your study and the more confident you want to be about cause and effect.

Measuring Reliability

There are four good methods of measuring reliability:

— test-retest

— multiple forms

— inter-rater

— split-half

The test-retest technique is to administer your test, instrument, survey, or measure to the same group of people at different points in time. Most researchers administer what is called a pretest for this, and to troubleshoot bugs at the same time. All reliability estimates are usually in the form of a correlation coefficient, so here, all you do is calculate the correlation coefficient between the two scores on the same group and report it as your reliability coefficient.

The multiple forms technique has other names, such as parallel forms and disguised test-retest, but it's simply the scrambling or mixing up of questions on your survey, for example, and giving it to the same group twice. The idea is that it's a more rigorous test of reliability.

Inter-rater reliability is most appropriate when you use assistants to do interviewing or content analysis for you. To calculate this kind of reliability, all you do is report the percentage of agreement on the same subject between your raters, or assistants. Split-half reliability is estimated by taking half of your test, instrument, or survey, and analyzing that half as if it were the whole thing. Then, you compare the results of this analysis with your overall analysis.

There are different variations of this technique, one of the most common being called Cronbach's alpha (a frequently reported reliability statistic) which correlates performance on each item with overall score. Another technique, closer to the split-half method, is the Kuder-Richardson coefficient, or KR-20. Statistical packages on most computers will calculate these for you, although in graduate school, you'll have to do them by hand and understand that all test statistics are derived from the formula that all observed scores consist of a true score and error score.

Estimating Validity

There are four good methods of estimating validity:

— face

— content

— criterion

— construct

Face validity is the least statistical estimate (validity overall is not as easily quantified as reliability) as it's simply an assertion on the researcher's partclaiming that they've reasonably measured what they intended to measure. It's essentially a "take my word for it" kind of validity. Usually, a researcher asks a colleague or expert in the field to vouch for the items measuring what they were intended to measure.

Content validity goes back to the ideas of conceptualization and operationalization. If the researcher has focused in too closely on only one type or narrow dimension of a construct or concept, then it's conceivable that other indicators were overlooked. In such a case, the study lacks content validity. Content validity is making sure you've covered all the conceptual space. There are different ways to estimate it, but one of the most common is a reliability approach where you correlate scores on one domain or dimension of a concept on your pretest with scores on that domain or dimension with the actual test.

Another way is to simply look over your inter-item correlations. Criterion validity is using some standard or benchmark that is known to be a good indicator. A researcher might have devised a police cynicism scale, for example, and they compare their Cronbach's alpha to the known Cronbach's alpha of say, Neiderhoffer's cynicism scale. There are different forms of criterion validity: concurrent validity is how well something estimates actual day-by-day behavior; predictive validity is how well something estimates some future event or manifestation that hasn't happened yet.

The latter type is commonly found in criminology. Suppose you are creating a scale that predicts how and when juveniles become mass murderers. To establish predictive validity, you would have to find at least one mass murderer, and investigate if the predictive factors on your scale, retrospectively, affected them earlier in life. With criterion validity, you're concerned with how well your items are determining your dependent variable.

Construct validity is the extent to which your items are tapping into the underlying theory or model of behavior. It's how well the items hang together or distinguish different people on certain traits or behaviors. It's the most difficult validity to achieve. You have to either do years and years of research or find a group of people to test that have the exact opposite traits or behaviors you're interested in measuring.

Threats Reliability and Validity

- *Ambiguity*: when correlation is taken for causation
- *Apprehension*: when people are scared to respond to your study
- *Compensation*: when a planned group or people contrast breaks down
- *Demoralization*: when people get bored with your measurements
- *Diffusion*: when people figure out your test and start mimicking symptoms
- *History*: when some critical event occurs between pretest and posttest
- *Inadeqate operationalization*: unclear definitions
- *Instrumentation*: when the researcher changes the measuring device
- *Interaction*: when confounding treatments or influences are co-occuring
- *Maturation*: when people change or mature over the research period
- *Mono-operation bias*: when using only one exemplar
- *Mortality*: when people die or drop out of the research
- *Regression to the mean*: a tendency toward middle scores
- *Rivalry*: the John Henry Effect, when groups compete to score good

— *Selection*: when volunteers are used, people self-select themselves

— *Setting*: something about the setting or context contaminates the study

— *Treatment*: the Hawthorne Effect, when people are trying to gain attention.

7

Research Design

The goal of research design is internal validity. A research design is said to be internally valid when it satisfies all three conditions of causality. Research design is a process a researcher undertakes in the beginning stages of research. To the extent that the researcher is trying to establish a causal relationship, he will choose a research design that best enables him to "prove" causality. As we shall see, some research designs are stronger than others in terms of meeting the conditions required by internal validity.

Experimental Research Design

Experiments are the Cadillacs or top guns of research design, the most expensive and powerful techniques you can use. Before even considering an experimental design, you need to ask the following:

- — Is it possible to precisely categorize the people, places, or things in your study?
- — Is is possible to select random people, places, or things in your study?
- — Is the process of random selection into experimental and control groups ethical and legal?

Experimental designs are rarely used in the social sciences for the third reason above. The subjects we often use are defendants, prisoners, or targeted populations, and it's either unethical or illegal to benefit one group while depriving another group of the treatment.

You can get away with experiments in other social sciences, like education and psychology, if you're experimenting with relatively harmless educational techniques or some simple perception or memory test. In general, if there's any risk of harm from delivering or withholding services to anybody in your sample, you cannot use an experimental design.

In those situations where you can use an experimental design, there are certain procedures you need to follow. First of all, you need to randomly select a control group, which is the same thing as a comparison group. This group must be statistically equal to the other group, a randomly assigned treatment group. Both groups must come from the same population, and "statistically equal" means that, even though selection was by randomization, you apply your knowledge of population characteristics to ensure that matching has occurred so that any extreme case in one group has a match or counterpart in the other group.

Randomization will take care of some of this for you, as will ad-hoc statistical controls, but the procedure known as matching will take you a lot further. Matched subjects, or subjects, in the control group are NOT to be exposed to some treatment, intervention, or change that you introduce or manipulate. You can have more than one control and treatment group. You can have full and partial treatment groups, or treatment groups based on different variations of some treatment, intervention, or change.

It's important that all your groups have about the same number of subjects in them, and as a general rule, you should have no less than 25 subjects in each group.

You should also conduct a pretest on your dependent variable, at least, across all groups to develop a statistical baseline. The experiment is complete when you take a final measure, called the posttest, but you can make multiple posttests at any time during the experiment. Your findings should be interpreted primarily from differences in a posttest score between experimental and control groups.

The term blind experiment means that you've gone out of your way to make sure the subjects don't know which group they're in, the experimental or control group. The term double blind experiment means that you and your research helpers don't even know who's in what group. These precautions help protect your study from the Hawthorne Effect and the Placebo Effect.

The Hawthorne effect refers to the tendency of subjects to act differently when they know they are being studied, especially if they think they have been singled out from some experimental treatment. The Placebo effect refers to the tendency of some subjects to think they are "cured" or sufficiently treated when they know about the research. By using placebos in your control group, you can neutralize or balance out the Hawthorne Effect, as well as possibly satisfy some ethical and legal qualms about withholding services from a control group.

The choice of which research design to use is related to the manifestation of the phenomenon within the population. The appropriateness of a design is also associated with a number of across-the-board concerns that affect your research from beginning to end.

Criminal justice is one of those fields where you rarely find experimental designs, for the third reason above. The subjects we often use are defendants, prisoners, or agency personnel, and it's either unethical or illegal to benefit one group while depriving another group of the treatment. You can get away with experiments in other social sciences, like education and psychology, if you're experimenting with relatively harmless educational techniques or some simple perception or memory test.

In general, if there's any risk of harm from delivering or withholding services to anybody in your sample, you cannot use an experimental design. In those situations where you can use an experimental design, there are certain procedures you need to follow. First of all, you need to randomly select a control group. This group must be statistically equal to the other group, a randomly assigned treatment group.

Both groups must come from the same population, and "statistically equal" means that, even though selection was by randomization, you apply your knowledge of population characteristics to ensure that matching has occurred so that any extreme case in one group has a match or counterpart in the other group. Randomization will take care of some of this for you, as will ad-hoc statistical controls, but the procedure known as matching will take you a lot further.

Matched subjects, or subjects, in the control group are not to be exposed to some treatment, intervention, or change that you introduce or manipulate. You can have more than one control and treatment group. You can have full and partial treatment groups, or treatment groups based on different variations of some treatment, intervention, or change. It's important that all your groups have about the same number of subjects in them, and as a general rule, you should have no less than 25 subjects in each group.

You should also (as a matter of ritual) conduct a pretest on your dependent variable, at least, across all groups to develop a statistical baseline. The experiment is complete when you take a final measure, called the posttest, but you can make multiple posttests at any time during the experiment. Your findings should be interpreted primarily from differences in a posttest score between experimental and control groups.

The term blind experiment means that you've gone out of your way to make sure the subjects don't know which group they're in, the experimental or control group. The term double blind experiment means that you and your research helpers don't even know who's in what group. These precautions help protect your study from the Hawthorne Effect and the Placebo Effect.

The Hawthorne effect refers to the tendency of subjects to act differently when they know they are being studied, especially if they think they have been singled out from some experimental treatment. The Placebo effect refers to the tendency of some subjects to think they are "cured" or sufficiently treated when they know about the research. By using placebos in your control group, you can neutralize or balance out the Hawthorne Effect, as well as possibly satisfy some ethical and legal qualms about withholding services from a control group. The choice of which research design to use is related to the manifestation of the phenomenon within the population.

QUASI-EXPERIMENTS

The word "quasi" means as if or almost, so a quasi-experiment means almost a true experiment. There are many varieties of quasi-experimental research designs, and there is generally little loss of status or prestige in doing a quasi-experiment instead of a true experiment, although you occasionally run into someone who is biased against quasi-experiments. Some common characteristics of quasi-experiments include the following:

— matching instead of randomization is used. For example, someone studying the effects of a new police strategy in town would try to find a similar town somewhere in the same geographic region, perhaps in a 5-state area. That other town would have citizen demographics that are very similar to the experimental town. That other town is not technically a control group, but a comparison group, and this matching strategy is sometimes called nonequivalent group design.

— time series analysis is involved. A time series is perhaps the most common type of longitudinal (over time) research found in criminal justice. A time series can be interrupted or noninterrupted. Both types examine changes in the dependent variable over time, with only an interrupted time series involving before and after measurement. For example, someone might use a time series to look at crime rates as a new law is taking effect. This kind of research is sometimes called impact analysis or policy analysis.

— the unit of analysis is often something different than people. Of course, any type of research can study anything - people, cars, crime statistics, neighborhood blocks. However, quasi-experiments are well suited for "fuzzy" or contextual concepts such as sociological quality of life, anomie, disorganization, morale, climate, atmosphere, and the like. This kind of research is sometimes called contextual analysis.

One of the intended purposes for doing quasi-experimental research is to capture longer time periods and a sufficient number of different events to control for various threats to validity and reliability. The hope is that the design will generate stable, reliable findings and tell us something about the effects of time itself. In fact, for a noninterrupted time series, the independent variable is usually time itself, for example, if you were monitoring rises and falls in crime rates and attributing it to changes in society over time.

Almost all quasi-experiments are somewhat creative or unusual in what they attribute the cause of something to, and this is the case because we aren't using a true experiment where we manipulate some independent variable in order to assess causality. Instead, at best, we have a statistical baseline and some interventions that have occurred naturally or were created by the researcher.

In quasi-experiments, the word "trend" is used instead of cause, and we are interested in finding the one true trend. Unfortunately, this kind of research often uncovers several trends, and the major ones are usually developed into "syndromes" or "cycles" while the minor ones are just referred to as normal or abnormal events. Say, for example, during the course of your research a bunch of college students from Florida State on spring break descended upon your town and started partying wildly.

You might call this the "Florida State syndrome" or something like that. Say, for example, a series of full moons came close together during the course of your study. You might call this the "full moon cycle." The point is that neither of these would be the true trend, but they might be trends nonetheless. Because quasi-experimental research designs tend to involve many different, but interlocking relationships between variables, it's advisable that the researcher engage in modeling the causal relationships.

This allows identification of spurious and intervening variables, as well as a number of other variable relationship types like suppression effects. Spurious variables should be thrown out; intervening variables require multiplying the effects of two variables (interaction terms); and suppression refers to when part of a variable affects part of another variable even though the bivariate relationship is nonsignificant. Models also permit elaboration and specification.

Elaboration is the process of reclassifying or subclassifying your variables, sometimes even switching around your independent and dependent variables. Specification is the process of making your dependent variable more narrow (e.g., applies only to left-handed, lower-class black males) and then multiplying some of your independent variables into a new, more powerful interaction term which has to be interpreted as some new kind of variable, not the additive sum of the original variables.

A variety of causal modeling techniques exist, from the fairly simple use of crosstabulation tables to run partial correlation analysis to the more sophisticated, and rarely-seen technique of path analysis which is essentially a regression run of each variable on every other variable. In some undergraduate courses like this, students sometimes analyze crosstabs for almost the whole semester; that's how important some instructors think modeling is as a heuristic device for teaching research methods.

Non- experimental Design

Non-experimental designs are generally referred to as correlational deisgns or cross-sectional designs. These are the main type of research designs employed in the social sciences. Correlational studies examine the relationship between two or more variables at a single point in time. Data is collected on both the independent and dependent variables from the same time period in order to determine if there is a relationship.

For example, if we wanted to find out whether SAT scores determine success in college, we could use a correlational design. Similarily, if we wished to study whether peoples' ages affect their opinion on whether marijuana should be legalized or not, we could use a correlational study. The correlation coefficient, also known as Pearson's R, is the principal statistical measure we use in correlational studies. Pearson's R ranges in value from 1 to -1.

It measures the strength and direction of the relationship between the independent and dependent variables. For example, a Pearson's R of .5 indicates that there is a moderately strong and positive relationship between the independent variable and the dependent variable. Or, an increase or a decrease in the independent variable "causes" a moderate increase or decrease in the dependent variable. Pearson's R measures the extent to which both the independent and dependent variables covary, or change together. It is not a measure of causality.

Besides the correlation coefficient, the coefficient of determination, r2, allows us to measure the precise amount of change in the dependent variable that is "caused by" a change in the independent variable. Let's say we are exploring the relationship between industrialization and infant mortality. We obtain data on each of our variables and conduct a regression analysis. We obtain an R value of .6. To find the coefficient of determination, we square Pearson's R, which would be .36.

We can now say that 36% of the change in infant mortality is explained by changes in levels of industrialization. The other 64% change in infant mortality is explained by other unknown factors. The coefficient of determination is the preferred statistic since it is the amount of change in the dependent variable that we are always interested in. That is, we are always interested in finding the best explanation for the change in the dependent variable.

Correlational studies are useful in trying to establish relationships between certain individual characteristics, e.g. education, income, race, age, gender, etc. and some observed behavior, such as political participation, opinions on social and political issues, and the like. If one wanted to find out whether men or women are more supportive of gun control legislation, a correlational study would be appropriate. Now if we wanted to see whether gun control legislation had in fact reduced the number of accidental shootings in a given year, what kind of research design would be set up?.

Not a correlational design because we are now looking at shootings over time. To see whether the legislation had an effect, we have to compare the number of shooting before and after the law was changed. Therefore, we would use a quasi-experimental design (an interrupted time series). Correlational studies based on individual observations frequently allow us to generalize to group behavior. For example, a correlational study of the relationship between age and voter turnout might allow us to make the following generalization: The younger people are, the less likely they are to vote.

Correlational designs are relatively easy and inexpensive to carry out. Their limitation is that they are very weak in terms of establishing causality. The most one can say is that there is a relationship either weak, moderate or strong, and whether it is positive or negative.

8

Data Analysis

The terms "statistics" and "data analysis" mean the same thing – the study of how we describe, combine, and make inferences from numbers. A lot of people are scared of numbers (quantiphobia), but statistics has got less to do with numbers, and more to do with rules for arranging them. In social science, that may seem like all that's necessary, since we're studying the obvious anyway.

However, there's a difference between something socially, or meaningfully significant, and something statistically significant. Statistical significance is first of all, short and simple. You communicate as much with just one number as a paragraph of description. Some people don't like statistics because of this reductionism, but it's become the settled way researchers communicate with one another. Secondly, statistical significance is what policy and decision making is based on.

Policymakers will dismiss anything nonstatistical as anecdotal evidence. Anecdotal means interesting and amusing, but hardly serious enough to be published or promulgated. Finally, just because something is statistically significant doesn't make it true. It's better than guessing, but you can lie and deceive with statistics. Since they can mislead you, there's no substitute for knowing something about the topic so that, as is the most common interpretative approach, the researcher is able to say what is both meaningful and statistically significant.

There are three (3) general areas that make up the field of statistics: descriptive statistics, relational statistics, and inferential statistics.

— *Descriptive statistics fall into one of two categories*: measures of central tendency (mean, median, and mode) or measures of dispersion (standard deviation and variance). Their purpose is to explore hunches that may have come up during the course of the research process, but most people compute them to look at the normality of their numbers. Examples include descriptive analysis of sex, age, race, social class, and so forth.

— *Relational statistics fall into one of three categories*: univariate, bivariate, and multivariate analysis. Univariate analysis is the study of one variable for a subpopulation, for example, age of murderers, and the analysis is often descriptive, but you'd be surprised how many advanced statistics can be computed using just one variable. Bivariate analysis is the study of a relationship between two variables, for example, murder and meanness, and the most commonly known technique here is correlation.

  Multivariate analysis is the study of relationship between three or more variables, for example, murder, meanness, and gun ownership, and for all techniques in this area, you simply take the word "multiple" and put it in front of the bivariate technique used, as in multiple correlation.

— *Inferential statistics, also called inductive statistics, fall into one of two categories*: tests for difference of means and tests for statistical significance, the latter which are further subdivided into parametric or nonparametric, depending upon whether you're inferring to the larger population as a whole (parametric) or the people in your sample (nonparametric). The purpose of difference of means tests is to test hypotheses, and the most common techniques are called Z-tests. The most common parametric tests of significance are the F-test, t-test, ANOVA, and regression.

The most common nonparametric tests of significance are chi-square, the Mann-Whitney U-test, and the Kruskal-Wallis test. To summarize:

— Descriptive statistics (mean, median, mode; standard deviation, variance)

— Relational statistics (correlation, multiple correlation)

— Inferential tests for difference of means (Z-tests)

— Inferential parametric tests for significance (F-tests, t-tests, ANOVA, regression)

— Inferential nonparametric tests for significance (chi-square, Mann-Whitney, Kruskal-Wallis)

Measure of Central Tendency

The most commonly used measure of central tendency is the mean. To compute the mean, you add up all the numbers and divide by how many numbers there are. It's not the average nor a halfway point, but a kind of center that balances high numbers with low numbers. For this reason, it's most often reported along with some simple measure of dispersion, such as the range, which is expressed as the lowest and highest number.

The median is the number that falls in the middle of a range of numbers. It's not the average; it's the halfway point. There are always just as many numbers above the median as below it. In cases where there is an even set of numbers, you average the two middle numbers. The median is best suited for data that are ordinal, or ranked.

It is also useful when you have extremely low or high scores.

The mode is the most frequently occurring number in a list of numbers. It's the closest thing to what people mean when they say something is average or typical. The mode doesn't even have to be a number. It will be a category when the data are nominal or qualitative. The mode is useful when you have a highly skewed set of numbers, mostly low or mostly high. You can also have two modes (bimodal distribution) when one group of scores are mostly low and the other group is mostly high, with few in the middle.

Measure of Dispersion

In data analysis, the purpose of statistically computing a measure of dispersion is to discover the extent to which scores differ, cluster, or spread from around a measure of central tendency. The most commonly used measure of dispersion is the standard deviation. You first compute the variance, which is calculated by subtracting the mean from each number, squaring it, and dividing the grand total by how many numbers there are. The square root of the variance is the standard deviation.

The standard deviation is important for many reasons. One reason is that, once you know the standard deviation, you can standardize by it. Standardization is the process of converting raw scores into what are called standard scores, which allow you to better compare groups of different sizes. Standardization isn't required for data analysis, but it becomes useful when you want to compare different subgroups in your sample, or between groups in different studies.

A standard score is called a z-score (not to be confused with a z-test), and is calculated by subtracting the mean from each and every number and dividing by the standard deviation. Once you have converted your data into standard scores, you can then use probability tables that exist for estimating the likelihood that a certain raw score will appear in the population. This is an example of using a descriptive statistic (standard deviation) for inferential purposes.

CORRELATION

The most commonly used relational statistic is correlation, and it's a measure of the strength of some relationship between two variables, not causality. Interpretation of a correlation coefficient does not even allow the slightest hint of causality.

The most a researcher can say is that the variables share something in common; that is, are related in some way. The more two things have something in common, the more strongly they are related. There can also be negative relations, but the important quality of correlation coefficients is not their sign, but their absolute value. A correlation of -.58 is stronger than a correlation of .43, even though with the former, the relationship is negative. The interpretations for various correlation coefficients:

.8 to 1.0	very strong
.6 to .8	strong
.4 to .6	moderate
.2 to .4	weak
.0 to .2	very weak

The most frequently used correlation coefficient in data analysis is the Pearson product moment correlation. It is symbolized by the small letter r, and is fairly easy to compute from raw scores using the following formula:

$$r = \frac{N\Sigma xy - (\Sigma x)(\Sigma y)}{\sqrt{[N\Sigma x^2 - (\Sigma x)^2][N\Sigma y^2 - (\Sigma y)^2]}}$$

Where:

N	=	number of pairs of scores
Σxy	=	sum of the products of paired scores
Σx	=	sum of x scores
Σy	=	sum of y scores
Σx^2	=	sum of squared x scores
Σy^2	=	sum of squared y scores

If you square the Pearson correlation coefficient, you get the coefficient of determination, symbolized by the large letter R. It is the amount of variance accounted for in one variable by the other. Large R can also be computed by using the statistical technique of regression, but in that situation, it's interpreted as the amount of variance explained for one variable by another. If you subtract a coefficient of determination from one, you get something called the coefficient of alienation, which is sometimes seen in the literature.

Z-Tests, F- Tests, and T- Tests

These refer to a variety of tests for inferential purposes. Z-tests are not to be confused with z-scores. Z-tests come in a variety of forms, the most popular being:

— to test the significance of correlation coefficients;

— to test for equivalence of sample proportions to population proportions, as in whether the number of minorities you've got in your sample is proportionate to the number in the population. Z-tests essentially check for linearity and normality, allow some rudimentary hypothesis testing, and allow the ruling out of Type I and Type II error.

F-tests are much more powerful, as they allow explanation of variance in one variable accounted for by variance in another variable. In this sense, they are very much like the coefficient of determination. One really needs a full-fledged statistics course to gain an understanding of F-tests, so suffice it to say here that you find them most commonly with regression and ANOVA techniques. F-tests require interpretation by using a table of critical values.

T-tests are kind of like little F-tests, and similar to Z-tests. It's appropriate for smaller samples, and relatively easy to interpret since any calculated t over 2.0 is, by rule of thumb, significant. T-tests can be used for one sample, two samples, one tail, or two-tailed. You use a two-tailed test if there's any possibility of bidirectionality in the relationship between your variables. The formula for the t-test is as follows:

$$t = \frac{\bar{X}_T - \bar{X}_C}{\sqrt{\dfrac{var_1}{(n_1 - 1)} + \dfrac{var_2}{(n_2 - 1)}}}$$

Analysis of Variance (ANOVA)

Analysis of Variance (ANOVA) is a data analytic technique based on the idea of comparing explained variance with unexplained variance, kind of like a comparison of the coefficient of determination with the coefficient of alienation. It uses a rather unique computational formula which involves squaring almost every column of numbers.

What is called the Between Sum of Squares (BSS) refers to variance in one variable explained by variance in another variable, and what is called the Within Sum of Squares (WSS) refers to variance that is not explained by variance in another variable. A F-test is then conducted on the number obtained by dividing BSS by WSS. The results are presented in what's called an ANOVA source table, which looks like the following:

Source	SS	df	MS	F	p
Total	2800				
Between	1800	1	1800	10.80	<.05
Within	1000	6	166.67		

REGRESSION

Regression is the closest thing to estimating causality in data analysis, and that's because it predicts how much the numbers "fit" a projected straight line. There are also advanced regression techniques for curvilinear estimation. The most common form of regression, however, is linear regression, and the least squares method to find an equation that best fits a line representing what is called the regression of y on x.

The procedure is similar to computing a calculus minima. Instead of finding the perfect number, however, one is interested in finding the perfect line, such that there is one and only one line (represented by equation) that perfectly represents, or fits the data, regardless of how scattered the data points. The slope of the line (equation) provides information about predicted directionality, and the estimated coefficients (or beta weights) for x and y (independent and dependent variables) indicate the power of the relationship.

Use of a regression formula (not shown here because it's too large; only the generic regression equation is shown) produces a number called R-squared, which is a kind of conservative, yet powerful coefficient of determination. Interpretation of R-squared is somewhat controversial, but generally uses the same strength table as correlation coefficients, and at a minimum, researchers say it represents "variance explained."

$$y_i = \beta_0 + \beta_1 Z_i + e_i$$

where:

y_i = outcome score for the ith unit
β_0 = coefficient for the *intercept*
β_1 = coefficient for the *slope*
Z_i = 1 if i^{th} unit is in the treatment group
0 if i^{th} unit is in the control group
e_i = residual for the ith unit

CHI-SQUARE

A technique designed for less than interval level data is chi-square (pronounced kye- square), and the most common forms of it are the chi-square test for contingency and the chi-square test for independence. Other varieties exist, such as Cramer's V, Proportional Reduction in Error (PRE) statistics, Yule's Q, and Phi. Essentially, all chi-square type tests involve arranging the frequency distribution of the data in what is called a contingency table of rows and columns.

Marginals, which are estimates of error in predicting concordant pairs in the rows and columns (based on the null hypothesis), are then computed, subtracted from one another, and expressed in the form of a ratio, or contingency coefficient. Predicted scores based on the null hypothesis are called expected frequencies, and these are subtracted from observed frequencies (Observed minus Expected). Chi-square tests are frequently seen in the literature, and can be easily done by hand, or are run by computers automatically whenever a contingency table is asked for.

The chi-square test for contingency is interpreted as a strength of association measure, while the chi-square test for independence (which requires two samples) is a nonparametric test of significance that essentially rules out as much sampling error and chance as possible.

Mann-Whitney and Kruskal-Wallis Tests

The Mann-Whitney U test is similar to chi-square and the t-test, and used whenever you have ranked ordinal level measurement. As a significance test, you need two samples, and you rank (say, from 1 to 15) the scores in each group, looking at the number of ties. A z-table is used to compare calculated and table values of U. The interpretation is usually along the lines of some significant difference being due to the variables you've selected.

The Kruskal-Wallis H test is similar to ANOVA and the F-test, and also uses ordinal, multisample data. It's most commonly seen when raters are used to judge research subjects or research content. Rank calculations are compared to a chi-square table, and interpretation is usually along the lines that there are some significant differences, and grounds for accepting research hypotheses.

Understanding Statistical Interpretation

P-value: A p-value, sometimes called an uncertainty or probability coefficient, is based on properties of the sampling distribution. It is usually expressed as p less than some decimal, as in $p < .05$ or $p < .0006$, where the decimal is obtained by tweaking the significance setting of any statistical procedure you run in SPSS. It is used in two ways:

— as a criterion level where you, the researcher have arbitrarily decided in advance to use as the cutoff where you reject the null hypothesis, in which case, you would ordinarily say something like "setting p at p > .65 for one-tailed or two-tailed tests of significance allows some confidence that 65% of the time, rejecting the null hypothesis will not be in error"; and more commonly,

— as a expression of inference uncertainty after you have run some test statistic regarding the strength of some association or relationship between your independent and dependent variables, in which case, you would say something like "the evidence suggests there is a statistically significant effect, however, p < .05 also suggests that 5% of the time, we should be uncertain about the significance of drawing any statistical inferences."

Mean: The mean, or average, is a word describing the average calculated over an entire population. It is therefore a parameter, and the average in a sample is both a descriptive statistic and your best estimate of the population mean. The best way to describe it is as: "a mean of 22.5 indicates that the average score in this sample and by inference the population as a whole is 22.5".

Standard deviation: The standard deviation represents a set of numbers indicating the spread, or typical distance between a single number and the set's average. A standard deviation value of 15, for example, would be interpreted as: "a mean of 22.5 and standard deviation of 15 means that the most typical number of cases fall into a range from 7.5 to 37.5".

Standard error: The standard error is the standard deviation of a sampling distribution. It is your best guess about the size of a difference between a statistic used to estimate a parameter and the parameter itself. As an expression of uncertainty, it has two advantages over the p-value:

— something called degrees of freedom are always associated with it; and

— it is used in the calculation of other, more advanced statistics. The number of degrees of freedom for purposes of calculating the standard error is always N - 1, or the total number of cases in your sample minus one.

The number of degrees of freedom for analyzing residuals is always N-2, or the total number of cases in your sample minus two. As you apply other, more advanced statistics, the same pattern holds with progressively more subtracted from your total sample size. Since you generally don't want large degrees of freedom, it may be better for you, the researcher, to think the opposite way, that is, to look at the way you measured your variables (both independent - the numerator; and dependent - the denominator) and think about how the subjects in your sample might have been confused and meant something else when they responded to items measuring your concept or construct.

If you used multiple measures, or several items measuring the same thing different ways, you generally won't have a problem, but if you measured "broken home" by divorce only, you may have as many as seven (7) different degrees of freedom for this concept because there are plenty of other ways a home could be broken.

Residual plot: A residual plot, or scattergram, is a diagnostic tool which the researcher normally uses to decide on what is called the robustness of any advanced statistic to be used later. Robustness is how well an advanced statistic can tolerate violations of the assumptions for its use. Statistics such as the t-test, the F-test, regression, and even correlation have many assumptions such as random sampling, independence across groups, nearly equivalent means, equal standard deviations, and the like.

Residuals are the original observations (the raw data) with any group averages subtracted, and this is done using transformations like Z-scores or studentized t-scores. The residuals (usually the x-axis) are then plotted against the group averages (usually the y-axis and called something like centertized values or leverage), and the resulting scatterplot of residuals versus group averages is then visually analyzed by the researcher to find ways to better further analysis. There are many things to look for in a scatterplot, the most important ones being:

— a funnel-shaped pattern would indicate the need for a log, exponential, or some other transformation of the raw data; and

— the presence of outliers, or seriously outlying observations, which might indicate throwing out a few cases in your sample.

Correlation: a Pearson's correlation coefficient, or small r, represents the degree of linear association between any two variables. Unlike regression, correlation doesn't care which variable is the independent one or the dependent one, therefore, you cannot infer causality. Correlations are also dimension-free, but they require a good deal of variability or randomness in your outcome measures. A correlation coefficient always ranges from negative one (-1) to one (1), so a negative correlation coefficient of -0.65 indicates that "65% of the time, when one variable is low, the other variable is high" and it's up to you, the researcher to guess which one is usually initially low.

A positive correlation coefficient of 0.65 indicates that "65% of the time, when one variable exerts a positive influence, the other variable also exerts a positive influence". Researchers often report the names of the variables in such sentences, rather than just saying "one variable". A correlation coefficient at zero, or close to zero, indicates no linear relationship.

F-test: The F-statistic is a test of significance used as an analysis of variance tool and also as a regression tool. It is used to test whether all, or several, statistical coefficients that can be calculated are zero or nonzero. It does this by calculating and comparing what are called generalized sum of squares, a principle that many statistics are based on. In the case of testing a single coefficient, the F-statistic is the square of the t-statistic, and they are interpreted similarly. F-statistics are compared to a table of numbers which contain values of expected F-distributions.

The degrees of freedom in the numerator are the number of coefficients tested (the number of independent variables being regressed); the denominator is the degrees of freedom associated with your standard error. By locating these spots in a table, you see if an F-statistic is greater than what can normally be expected in a F-distribution. If it is greater than what the table indicates, you can say that your full model (all your variables) have statistical significance.

This is often interpreted by saying: "A statistically significant F of .428 with an associated p-value of .66 indicates that 66% of the time, the variables selected for observation in this study will provide a good fit in explanatory models of the outcome being measured." Researchers normally substitute words for what the actual outcome is (crime, quality of life, etc.) instead of saying "the outcome being measured".

R-squared: The R-squared statistic, or the coefficient of determination, is the percentage of total response variation explained by the independent variables. Adjusted R-squared is preferable to use if you have a lot of independent variables since R-squared can always be made larger by adding more variables. R-squared statistics are usually interpreted as percentages, such as: "an R-squared of .51 indicates that fifty-one percent of the variation in is explained by a linear regression on." R-squared should be identical to the square of the sample correlation coefficient; that is R alone represents your multiple correlation coefficient. Adjusted R-squared represents a penalty for unnecessary variables.

Cook's distance: Cook's distance, or the d-statistic, represents overall influence, or the effect that omitting a case has on the estimated regression coefficients. A case that has a large Cook's distance will be a case that is influential if it is deleted. It may have a large d-statistic because it has a large studentized residual, a large leverage, or both. It is up to the researcher to determine what is causing such an influence, and whether or not the cases should be deleted or the whole dataset smoothed.

Durbin-Watson statistic: J. Durbin and G.S. Watson developed the DW statistic as a test for comparing how close residuals are to their past values and how close they are to their average. The test is usually done with time series data, and confirms or rejects evidence of serial correlation. With regression, a high DW statistic suggests there is independence of the observations, and that you, the researcher, can rule out various threats to validity like history, maturation, and decay.

Pitfalls of Data Analysis

The core value of statistical methodology is its ability to assist one in making inferences about a large group (a population) based on observations of a smaller subset of that group (a sample). In order for this to work correctly, a couple of things have to be true: the sample must be similar to the target population in all relevant aspects; and certain aspects of the measured variables must conform to assumptions which underlie the statistical procedures to be applied.

Representative sampling: This is one of the most fundamental tenets of inferential statistics: the observed sample must be representative of the target population in order for inferences to be valid. Of course, the problem comes in applying this principle to real situations. The ideal scenario would be where the sample is chosen by selecting members of the population at random, with each member having an equal probability of being selected for the sample. Barring this, one usually tries to be sure that the sample "parallels" the population with respect to certain key characteristics which are thought to be important to the investigation at hand, as with a stratified sampling procedure.

While this may be feasible for certain manufacturing processes, it is much more problematic for studying people. For instance, consider the construction of a job applicant screening instrument: the population about which you want to know something is the pool of all possible job applicants. You surely won't have access to the entire population--you only have access to a certain number of applicants who apply within a certain period of time. So you must hope that the group you happen to pick isn't somehow different from the target population.

An example of a problematic sample would be if the instrument were developed during an economic recession; it is reasonable to assume that people applying for jobs during a recession might be different as a group from those applying during a period of economic growth. In this case, you'd want to exercise caution when using the instrument during better economic times.

There are also ways to account for, or "control", differences between groups statistically, as with the inclusion of covariates in a linear model. Unfortunately, as Levin points out, there are problems with this approach, too. One can never be sure one has accounted for all the important variables, and inclusion of such controls depends on certain assumptions which may or may not be satisfied in a given situation.

Statistical assumptions: The validity of a statistical procedure depends on certain assumptions it makes about various aspects of the problem. For instance, well-known linear methods such as analysis of variance (ANOVA) depends on the assumption of normality and independence. The first of these is probably the lesser concern, since there is evidence that the most common ANOVA designs are relatively insensitive to moderate violations of the normality assumption.

Unfortunately, this offers an almost irresistible temptation to ignore any non-normality, no matter how bad the situation is. The robustness of statistical techniques only goes so far--"robustness" is not a license to ignore the assumption. If the distributions are non-normal, try to figure out why; if it's due to a measurement artifact (e.g. a floor or ceiling effect), try to develop a better measurement device (if possible).

Another possible method for dealing with unusual distributions is to apply a transformation. However, this has dangers as well; an ill-considered transformation can do more harm than good in terms of interpretability of results. The assumption regarding independence of observations is more troublesome, both because it underlies nearly all of the most commonly used statistical procedures, and because it is so frequently violated in practice.

Observations which are linked in some way – parts manufactured on the same machine, students in the same classroom, consumers at the same mall – all may show some dependencies. Therefore, if you apply some statistical test across students in different classrooms, say to assess the relationship between different textbook types and test scores, you're introducing bias into your results.

This occurs because, the kids in the class presumably interact with each other, chat, talk about the new books they're using, and so influence each other's responses to the test. This will cause the results of your statistical test (e.g. correlations or p-values) to be inaccurate. One way to try to get around this is to aggregate cases to the higher level, e.g. use classrooms as the unit of analysis, rather than students.

Unfortunately this requires sacrificing a lot of statistical power, making a Type II error more likely. Happily, methods have been developed recently which allow simultaneous modeling of data which is hierarchically organized. One of the papers presented at this conference introduces these methods. Additionally, interested readers are referred to Bryk & Raudenbush and Goldstein for good overviews of these hierarchical models.

Errors in Methodology

There are a number of ways that statistical techniques can be misapplied to problems in the real world. Three of the most common hazards are designing experiments with insufficient power,ignoring measurement error, and performing multiple comparisons.

Statistical Power: This topic has become quite in vogue lately, at least in the academic community; indeed, some federal funding agencies seem to consider any research proposal incomplete unless it contains a comprehensive power analysis. This graph will help illustrate the concept of power in an experiment. In the figure, the vertical dotted line represents the point-null hypothesis, and the solid vertical line represents a criterion of significance, i.e. the point at which you claim a difference is significant.

Recall that there are two types of errors which can occur when making inferences based on a statistical hypothesis test: a Type I error occurs if you reject the null hypothesis when you shouldn't (the probability of this is what we call "alpha", and is indicated by the cross-hatched region of the graph); a Type II error occurs if you don't reject it when you should.

Power refers to the probability of avoiding a Type II error, or, more colloquially, the ability of your statistical test to detect true differences of a particular size. The power of your test generally depends on four things: your sample size, the effect size you want to be able to detect, the Type I error rate (alpha) you specify, and the variability of the sample. Based on these parameters, you can calculate the power level of your experiment.

Or, as is most commonly done, you can specify the power you desire, the alpha level, and the minimum effect size which you would consider "interesting", and use the power equation to determine the proper sample size for your experiment.

Now, if you have too little power, you run the risk of overlooking the effect you're trying to find. This is especially important if you intend to make inferences based on a finding of no difference. This is what allows advertisers to claim "No brand is better at relieving headaches (or what have you)"--if they use a relatively small sample, of course any differences in pain relief won't be significant. The differences may be there, but the test used to look for them was not sensitive enough to find them.

While the main emphasis in the development of power analysis has been to provide methods for assessing and increasing power, it should also be noted that it is possible to have too much power. If your sample is too large, nearly any difference, no matter how small or meaningless from a practical standpoint, will be "statistically significant". This can be particularly problematic in applied settings, where courses of action are determined by statistical results.

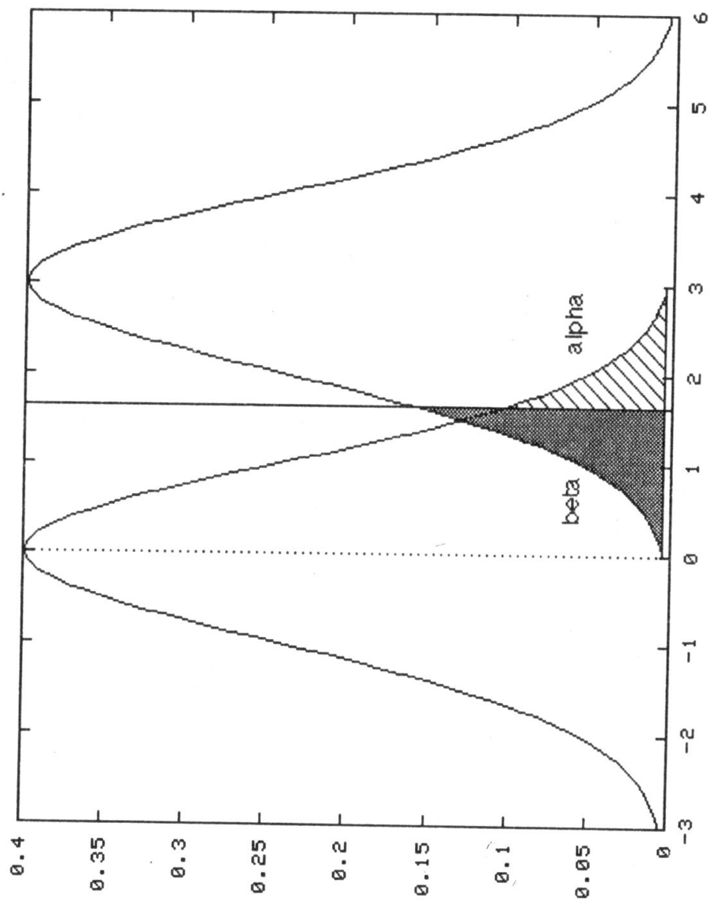

Figure 1. Illustration of the concept of power in an experiment

Multiple comparisons: This is a particularly thorny issue, because often what we want to know about is complex in nature, and we really need to check a lot of different combinations of factors to see what's going on. However, doing so in a haphazard manner can be dangerous, if not downright disastrous. Remember that each comparison we make entails a Type I error risk equal to our predefined alpha. We might assign the conventional value of .05 to alpha. Each comparison we make has a (1 - .05) = .95 probability of avoiding a Type I error.

Now suppose we have 12 process variables, and we want to see what the relationships are among them. We might be tempted to calculate the 66 possible correlations, and see which ones turn out to be statistically significant. Here's where the fun begins: in the best-case scenario, where the comparisons are independent (not true for this example, but we'll assume it for the sake of argument), the probability of getting all the comparisons right is the product of the probabilities for getting each comparison right. In this case that would be (.95)^66, or about .03.

Thus your chance of getting all 66 comparisons right is almost zero. This figure shows the probability of getting one or more errors based on how many comparisons you make, assuming a per-comparison alpha of .05. In fact, if you were to take 12 completely uncorrelated variables (that is, take a sample from each of 12 uncorrelated variables) and calculate the set of 66 correlations, you should expect to see about 3 spurious correlations in each set. This figure shows the expected number of errors based on number of comparisons, assuming a nominal alpha of .05.

So, suppose you calculate your correlations and discover that 10 of them seem to be significant. You'll have a tough time sorting out which ones are real and which are spurious. Several strategies can be used to overcome this problem. The easiest, but probably the least acceptable,

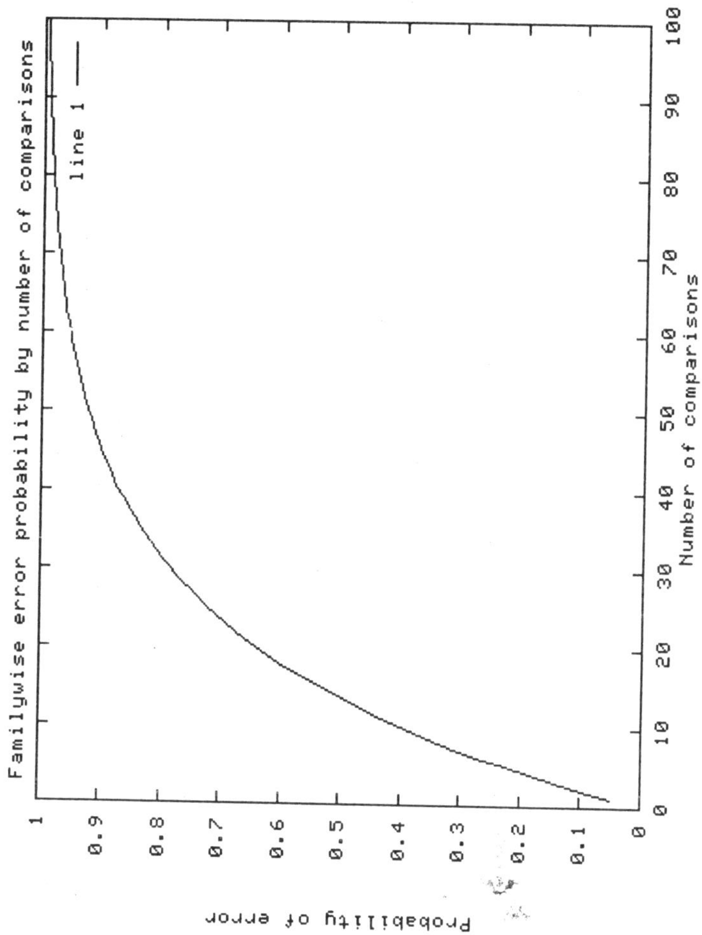

Figure 2. Probability of getting one or more errors based on many comparisons

is to adjust your alpha criterion (by making it smaller) so that the "familywise" error rate is what you'd like it to be.

The problem with this strategy is that it is impractical for large numbers of comparisons: as your alpha for each comparison becomes smaller, your power is reduced to almost nil. The best strategy, but usually an expensive one, is replication--rerun the experiment and see which comparisons show differences in both groups.

This is not quite foolproof, but it should give you a pretty good idea which effects are real and which are not. If you can't actually replicate, the next best thing is a technique called cross-validation, which involves setting aside part of your sample as a validation sample. You compute the statistics of interest on the main sample, and then check them against the validation sample to verify that the effects are real. Results that are spurious will usually be revealed by a validation sample.

Measurement error: Most statistical models assume error free measurement, at least of independent (predictor) variables. However, as we all know, measurements are seldom if ever perfect. Particularly when dealing with noisy data such as questionnaire responses or processes which are difficult to measure precisely, we need to pay close attention to the effects of measurement errors. Two characteristics of measurement which are particularly important in psychological measurement are reliability and validity.

Reliability refers to the ability of a measurement instrument to measure the same thing each time it is used. So, for instance, a reliable measure should give you similar results if the units (people, processes, etc.) being measured are similar. Additionally, if the characteristic being measured is stable over time, repeated measurement of the same unit should yield consistent results.

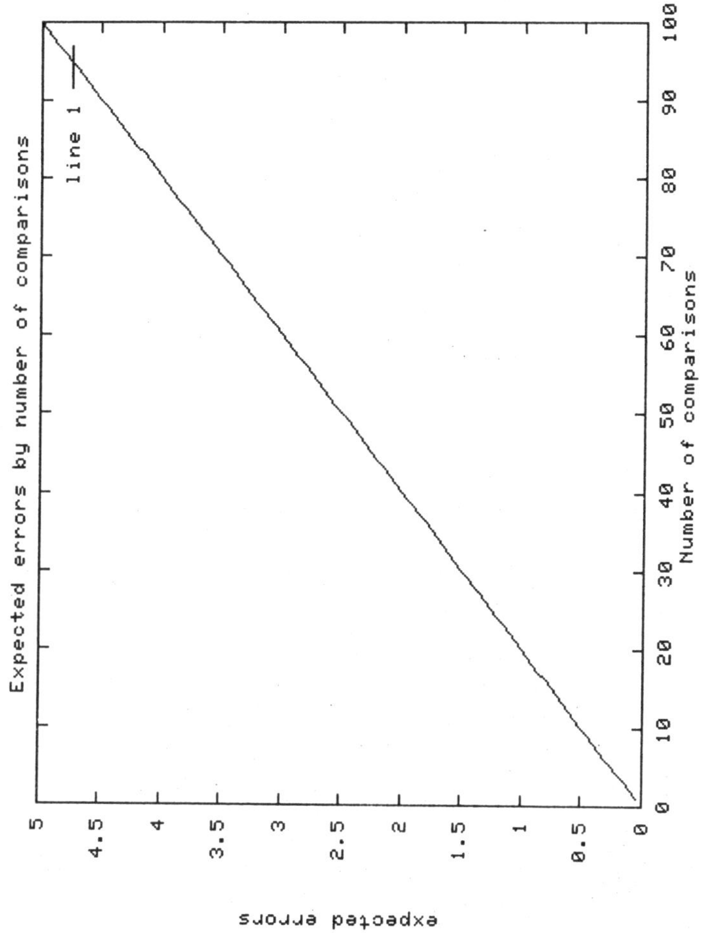

Figure 3. Expected number of errors based on number of comparisons

Validity is the extent to which the indicator measures the thing it was designed to measure. Thus, while IQ tests will have high reliability (in that people tend to achieve consistent scores across time), they might have low validity with respect to job performance (depending on the job). Validity is usually measured in relation to some external criterion, e.g. results on a job-applicant questionnaire might be compared with subsequent employee reviews to provide evidence of validity.

Methods are available for taking measurement error into account in some statistical models. In particular, structural equation modeling allows one to specify relationships between "indicators", or measurement tools, and the underlying latent variables being measured, in the context of a linear path model. For more information on structural equation modeling and its uses, see Bollen. There are a number of difficulties which can arise in the context of substantive interpretation as well. We go through all these elaborate procedures, chew up time on the mainframe, generate reams of output--eventually, we have to try to make some sense of it all in terms of the question at hand.

Confusion over significance: While this topic has been expounded upon by nearly every introductory statistics textbook, the difference between "significance" in the statistical sense and "significance" in the practical sense continues to elude many statistical dabblers and consumers of statistical results. There is still a strong tendency for people to equate stars in tables with importance of results.

"Oh, the p-value was less than .001--that's a really big effect," we hear our clients say. Significance (in the statistical sense) is really as much a function of sample size and experimental design as it is a function of strength of relationship. With low power, you may be overlooking a really useful relationship; with excessive power, you may be finding microscopic effects with no real practical value.

A reasonable way to handle this sort of thing is to cast results in terms of effect sizes – that way the size of the effect is presented in terms that make quantitative sense. Remember that a p-value merely indicates the probability of a particular set of data being generated by the null model--it has little to say about size of a deviation from that model .

Precision and Accuracy: These are two concepts which seem to get confused an awful lot, particularly by those who aren't mathematically inclined. It's a subtle but important distinction: precision refers to how finely an estimate is specified, whereas accuracy refers to how close an estimate is to the true value. Estimates can be precise without being accurate, a fact often glossed over when interpreting computer output containing results specified to the fourth or sixth or eighth decimal place.

Graphical Represenations: There are many ways to present quantitative results numerically, and it is easy to go astray (or to lead your audience astray, if you are less than scrupulous) by misapplying graphical techniques. Tufte's book, The Visual Display of Quantitative Information, gives a wealth of information and examples on how to construct good graphs, and how to recognize bad ones.

One of the principles Tufte introduces to indicate the relationship between the data and the graphic is a number he calls "the Lie Factor". This is simply the ratio of the difference in the proportion of the graphic elements versus the difference in the quantities they represent. Another key element in making informative graphs is to avoid confounding design variation with data variation. This means that changes in the scale of the graphic should always correspond to changes in the data being represented.

9

Qualitative Methods

Data can come in the form of words, images, impressions, gestures, or tones which represent real events or reality as it is seen symbolically or sociologically. Qualitative research uses unreconstructed logic to get at what is really real – the quality, meaning, context, or image of reality in what people actually do, not what they say they do.

Unreconstructed logic means that there are no step-by-step rules, that researchers ought not to use prefabricated methods or reconstructed rules, terms, and procedures that try to make their research look clean and neat. It is therefore difficult to define qualitative research since it doesn't involve the same terminology as ordinary science. The simplest definition is to say it involves methods of data collection and analysis that are nonquantitative. Another way of defining it is to say it focuses on "quality", a term referring to the essence or ambience of something.

Methods of Qualitative Research

Participant-Observation

Participant-Observation is the process of immersing yourself in the study of people you're not too different from. It is almost always done covertly, with the researcher never revealing their true purpose or identity. If it's a group you already know a lot about, you need to step back and take the perspective of a "martian", as if you were from a different planet and seeing things in a fresh light.

If it's a group you know nothing about, you need to become a "convert" and really get committed and involved. The more secretive and amorphous the group, the more you need participation. The more localized and turf-conscious the group, the more you need observation. It's customary in the literature to describe four roles:

— *Complete participation*: the researcher participates in deviant or illegal activities and goes on to actively influence the direction of the group

— *Participant as observer*: the researcher participates in deviant or illegal activities but does not try to influence the direction of the group

— *Observer as participant*: the researcher participates in a one-time deviant or illegal activity but then takes a back seat to any further activities

— *Complete observation*: the researcher is a member of the group but does not participate in any deviant or illegal activities

It's difficult to say which of these four roles are the most common, probably the middle two. The key point behind all of them is that the researcher must operate on two levels: becoming an insider while remaining an outsider. They must avoid becoming oversocialized, or "going native", as well as being personally revolted or repulsed by the group conduct.

Going native is sometimes described as giving up research and joining the group for life, but in most criminological circles, it means losing your objectivity and glorifying criminals. Generally, it takes time to carry out participant-observation, several weeks or months to 2-4 years. Gangs, hate groups, prostitutes, and drug dealers have all been studied by this method.

Ethnography

Ethnography is the process of describing a culture or way of life from a folk peoples' point of view. Another name for it is field research. The folk point of view is the idea of a universe in a dewdrop, each person a reflection of their culture in that all their gestures, displays, symbols, songs, sayings, and everything else has some implicit, tacit meaning for others in that culture.

It's the job of ethnography to establish the hidden inferences that distinguish, for example, a wink and a nod in any given culture. Numerous funding opportunities exist both abroad and domestically for ethnographic research. The ethnographic method involves observation and note taking. The anthropologist Clifford Geertz called it thick description. For about every half hour of observation, an ethnographic researcher would write notes for about two hours.

These notes would contain rich, detailed descriptions of everything that went on. There would be no attempt at summarizing, generalizing, or hypothesizing. The notes would capture as factual a description of the drama as possible to permit multiple interpretations, and most of all, to later infer cultural meaning. A coding procedure (much like content analysis) would be used later for this.

One of the assumptions of ethnography is naturalism, or leaving natural phenomenon alone. In essence, the researcher tries to be invisible. There are a variety of ways the researcher develops trust and rapport with the folk group in order to do this, to watch and listen carefully without being noticed. At some point, however, the researcher has to disengage, retreat to a private place, and take notes. The following are some standard rules for taking field notes:

- Take notes as soon as possible, and do not talk to anyone before note taking
- Count the number of times key words or phrases are used by members of the folk group
- Carefully record the order or sequence of events, and how long each sequence lasts
- Do not worry that anything is too insignificant; record even the smallest things
- Draw maps or diagrams of the location, including your movements and any reaction by others
- Write quickly and don't worry about spelling; devise your own system of punctuation
- Avoid evaluative judgments or summarizing; don't call something "dirty" for example, describe it
- Include your own thoughts and feelings in a separate section; your later thoughts in another section
- Always make backup copies of your notes and keep them in a separate location

Photography

Photography, or filmmaking, is ethnography with recording equipment. While many ethnographers would advocate staying away from such technology, it's hard to deny the benefits as an aid to recall, multiple interpretation, and reaching a wider audience. Ethnographic film reports on the homeless, for example, may be just what is needed to mobilize community action or public funding.

Little has been written on this new qualitative method, but it appears that the technique known as oral history is sometimes combined with it. Oral history is the recording of people speaking in their own words, about their life experiences, both public and private, in ways that are unavailable in writing. You'd be amazed at the things people say, and the nuances they can communicate, while in front of a videocamera. It's unfortunate that this method hasn't caught on in criminal justice or criminology.

Ethnomethodology

Ethnomethodology is the study of commonsense knowledge, and is an ethnographic technique popularized by the sociologist Harold Garfinkel in the late 1960s. It assumes a more active role for the researcher, one that involves "breaking up" the standard routines of folk groups in order to see how strongly and in what ways group members mobilize to restore the cultural order.

The researcher would do weird things, for example, at inappropriate times. One of the classic textbook examples is looking up at the ceiling in a crowded elevator. Some people would glance up to see what you're looking at; another person might ask what you're looking at; and yet another person might demonize you by saying "What's the matter, too good to ride the elevator with the rest of us?"

The whole idea is not to break the law or even the norms of social conduct, but just do silly little things that violate customs or folkways, which will most likely get you labeled as odd, eccentric, or a folk devil. The researcher is then in a better position to understand the fragile and fluid processes of social control, as well as the rules that people use for maintaining cultural boundaries. In spite of the great theoretical potential of this research method, it is not all that commonly used. In fact, since 1989, most people refer to refined versions of this method as conversation analysis or sociolinguistics.

Dramaturgical Interviewing

Dramaturgical Interviewing, or just plain dramaturgy, is a technique of doing research by role playing or play acting your own biases in some symbolic interaction or social performance. Interviewing is conversation with a purpose. Dramaturgy was popularized by the sociologist Erving Goffman in the early 1960s and is also associated with the pseudopatient study "On Being Sane in Insane Places" by Rosenhan in 1973.

Both researchers pretended to be mentally ill to find out what it's like in a psychiatric hospital. It's important to note that the acting out doesn't have to be deceptive. In fact, it's preferable if the researcher act out on a self-conscious awareness of their own bias, and just exaggerates a bit, in order to instigate a more emotional response from the person being interviewed.

Knowing your biases is different from bracketing those biases, the latter requiring not just an awareness, but being hard on yourself, and developing a special openness or frankness that is the hallmark of a dramaturgical researcher. At a minimum, you should examine yourself according to the following:

— your gender, age, ethnicity, religion, political party, and favorite psychological theory

— the ways in which these characteristics might bias you in your efforts at interviewing

— the ways in which you might counteract these biases

— the ways in which your efforts to counteract your biases might lead to other biases

Rapport and trust come from meeting the interviewee's expectations about ascribed and achieved characteristics (gender, age, race, mannerisms, etc.), and then the interview proceeds in a semi-directed manner with the interviewer (always self-consciously) acting out on some bias believed to be associated with their own characteristics or those of the interviewee (if different).

In the first case, the researcher is a dramaturgical performer; in the second case, a dramaturgical choreographer. The thing to focus on with this technique is the nonverbal body language, as it is believed that affective messages contained therein are more important than verbal messages. A debriefing session is usually held after the dramaturgical interview. This method is probably one of the most difficult qualitative methods as it's basis is in phenomenological theory, but it has many advocates who point to its therapeutic value for both interviewer and interviewee.

Sociometry

Sociometry is the measurement of social distance between group members. More precisely, it is the assessment of attractions and repulsions between individuals in a group and with the group structure as defined by feelings. The method was first established by the social psychologist J.L. Moreno in 1934, and to this day, always involves a graphical depiction of the structure of group relations called a sociogram. The procedure for constructing a sociogram begins with a questionnaire-based sociometric test which asks each group member the following:

— name two or three peers you like the most, like working with, or are your best friends

— name two or three peers you least like, dislike working with, or that you reject as friends

— rate every member of the group in terms of like or dislike on a 5-point scale

After the mean ratings are collated, and one has identified what social structures exist, the researcher then locates appropriate guides, informants, and gatekeepers to the group.

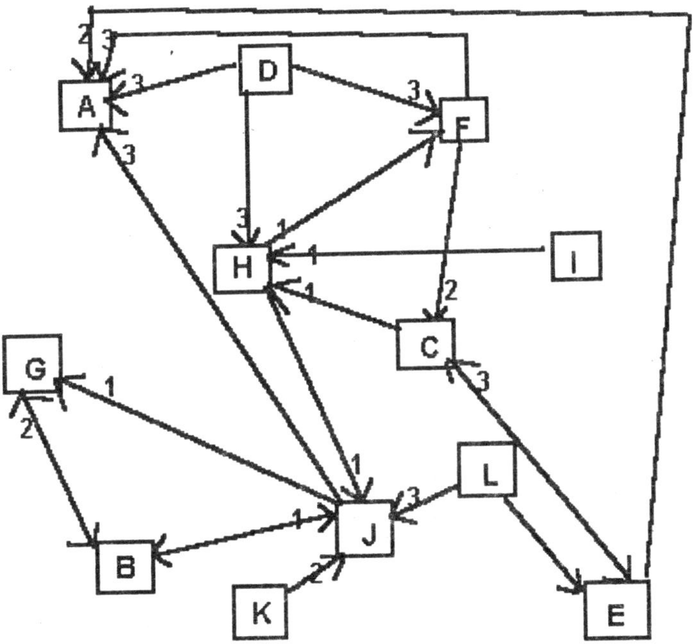

Figure 1. Measurement of Sociometry

Fieldwork, or ethnography, is engaged in to obtain field notes. Together with a coding and analysis of one's field notes and the collated results of sociometric testing, the researcher draws up a sociogram depicting star and satellite cliques, dyads, triads, and so forth. The arrows in the sociogram contain a number obtained by dividing an individual's column score by n-1. A summary table usually accompanies the sociogram showing the frequency distributions. An example of a sociogram appears above.

Natural Experiment

Natural Experiment refers to a situation where a split or

division has occurred between group members, and the researcher is afforded an opportunity to study the differentiation process of social structure. For example, suppose one group of students recruited by a college admissions staff received campus crime report cards in the mail, and another group did not. Both groups, however, had a chance to review a second report card once they got on campus.

The researcher could then survey or interview all of them once they got on campus, and not only make meaningful comparisons about the perceived helpfulness of first report card with the second, but inductive inferences about concern for crime and campus safety generally.

Natural experiments are frequently found in political science as tax codes change or federal legislation forces a state to change its welfare, workplace, education, or transportation policy. Increases or decreases in posted speed limits are natural experiments, for example.

In Historical-Comparative research, natural experiments occur when a nation switches from communism to capitalism. Economists use business booms and busts (recessions) as natural experiments. Unless the division has a random effect, interpretations from natural experiments are made in terms of qualitative factors, although a lot of "mathematizing" goes on. In recent years, researchers who rely on natural experiments have shown an interest in chaos theory.

Case Study

Case study occurs when all you have is information about one unique offender, and you want to generalize about all offenders of that type. The field of Justice Studies has been slower than Social Work and Clinical Psychology in embracing the value of a single-subject or case study approach.

Almost all case studies involve unstructured interview and ethnographic methodology. It's difficult to describe the variety of techniques used to arrive at useful generalizations in a case study. Hagan even covers a few quantitative techniques. One way to generalize from a sample of one is to argue that group data overlooks or blurs the significance of individual success or failure. Nomothetic (group) designs simply add up the totals and look at averages.

Idiographic (single subject) designs have the advantage of rescuing individual data from the pile of averages. This argument works best if the individual in question falls into some extreme category (successful at crime or a complete failure at it). Scientists refer to these cases as "outliers", and it is probably better to use someone successful than a failure. Studies of so-called successful, or able, criminals are especially useful at finding out how most offenders try to avoid detection by law enforcement.

Another way to generalize from a sample of one is to use the "universe in a dewdrop" argument we saw with ethnography. With case studies, this is called "methodological holism" and is quite common in Historical-Comparative research. The idea is to find a subject so average, so typical, so much like everyone else, that he/she seems to reflect the whole universe of other subjects around him/her. Anthropologists used to seek out the witchdoctor of a village, so you need to find someone who is a natural "storyteller".

Many offenders, if you can find one you believe to be articulate and truthful, have taken it upon themselves to chronicle, record, or otherwise keep an eye on the careers of others in their particular field of criminal behavior. These particular individuals will often pontificate on and on about what it's like to be someone like them, and some of them can be surprisingly accurate about it, even though they lack self-insight themselves. In order for this to be more than an exercise in typicality, you should use some standard protocol.

In other words, try to figure out which issues the subject regards as essential or worthwhile and which ones he/she regards as useless. You'll probably need some nonverbal behavior also. Several complex techniques exist for coding and analyzing the data, from content analysis to historiography to meta-ethnography, but a simple, old-fashioned Q-sort technique works well where you put the subject's different ideas down on 3x5 cards, lay them down on the floor, and shuffle them into 3-4 master categories (called "themes") that you make up the names for. Some standard categories might be:

— growing up a criminal;

— becoming a successful criminal;

— trying to stop being a criminal; and

— adjusting to the criminal life, but use your own creativity in naming the categories, and stay close to the actual statements by your subject.

Unobtrusive Measures

Unobtrusive Measures are ways of gathering data in which subjects are not aware of their being studied, and are sometimes called nonreactive measures. They usually involve clandestine, novel, or oddball collection of trace data that falls into one of two categories: accretion or erosion. Accretion is the stuff left behind by human activity. An example would be going through someone's garbage.

Erosion is the stuff that is worn down by human activity. An example would be examining wear and tear on floor tiles to estimate how much employees use the restroom. Examination of graffiti and vandalism are examples of unobtrusive measures in criminal justice. Nobody claims that unobtrusive measures are superior to other research methods. The only advantage is that it is useful when the subjects to be studied are very suspicious and distrustful.

Content Analysis

Content Analysis is a technique for gathering and analyzing the content of text. The content can be words, phrases, sentences, paragraphs, pictures, symbols, or ideas. It can be done quantitatively as well as qualitatively, and computer programs can be used to assist the researcher.

The initial step involves sorting the content into themes, which depends on the content. If you were studying white collar crime, for example, you might have themes like planning, action, and coverup. Then, a coding scheme is devised, usually in basic terms like frequency (amount of content), direction (who the content is directed to), intensity (power of content), and space (size of content). The coding system is used to reorganize the themed content in what is called manifest coding.

Manifest coding is highly reliable because you can train assistants to do it, ensuring intercoder reliability, and all you're doing is using an objective method to count the number of times a theme occurs in your coding scheme. At the next level, the researcher engages in what is called latent coding. This requires some knowledge, usually gained from fieldwork or observation, about the language rules, or semiotics, of your subjects. It is less reliable than manifest coding, but involves the researcher using some rubric or template to make judgment calls on implicit, ironic, or doubtful content.

Since not everything always fits in categories, there's always some leftover content to be accounted for, and it must be interpreted in context by a knowledgeable researcher who knows something about the culture of his/ her subjects. There are strict limitations on the inferences a researcher can make with content analysis. For example, inferences about motivation or intent can not normally be made, nor can the researcher infer what the effect of seeing such content would be on a viewer. Content analysis is only analysis of what is in the text. A researcher cannot use it to prove that newspapers intended, for example, to mislead the public, or that a certain style of journalism has a particular effect on public attitudes.

The most common inferences in content analysis make use of concepts like unconscious bias or unintended consequences, and these are not the same as saying intentional bias or intended effect. Content analysis has been applied extensively to all kinds of media: newspapers, magazines, television, movies, and the Internet. Intelligence and law enforcement agencies also do content analysis regularly on diplomatic channels of communication, overseas phone calls, and Internet emails.

A key point to remember is that the more quantitative aspects of content analysis come first; the qualitative part of the analysis comes last, although some advocates say the technique involves moving back and forth between quantitative and qualitative methods.

Historiography

Historiography is the method of doing historical research or gathering and analyzing historical evidence. There are four types of historical evidence: primary sources, secondary sources, running records, and recollections. Historians rely mostly on primary sources which are also called archival data because they are kept in museums, archives, libraries, or private collections.

Emphasis is given to the written word on paper, although modern historiography can involve any medium. Secondary sources are the work of other historians writing history. Running records are documentaries maintained by private or nonprofit organizations. Recollections are autobiographies, memoirs, or oral histories. Archival research, which is the most common, involves long hours of sifting through dusty old papers, yet inspection of untouched documents can yield surprising new facts, connections, or ideas.

Historiographers are careful to check and double-check their sources of information, and this lends a good deal of validity and reliability to their conclusions. Inferences about intent, motive, and character are common, with the understanding of appropriateness to the context of the time period. Historical-comparative researchers who do historiography often have to make even more disclaimers about meanings in context, such as how they avoided western bias.

Secondary Analysis

Secondary Analysis is the reanalysis of data that was originally compiled by another researcher for other purposes than the one the present researcher intends to use it for. Several datasets in criminal justice and criminology exist just for this purpose. The UCR (Uniform Crime Reports), for example, can be analyzed in a number of ways other than for its purpose as being a health scorecard for the nation. Often, secondary analysis will involve adding an additional variable to an existing dataset.

This variable will be something that the researcher collects on their own, from another dataset, or from a common source of information. For example, one could take police call for service data and combine it with lunar cycles from the Farmer's Almanac to study the effect of full moons on weird human behavior. Secondary data analysis is only limited by the researcher's imagination.

While the technique is mostly quantitative, limitations exist that often force such researchers to have some qualitative means of garnering information also. In such cases, the qualitative part of the study is used as a validity check on the quantitative part. A related technique, called meta-analysis, is the combining the results of several different studies dealing with the same research question. It is decidedly quantitative, but involves some of the same sorting and coding techniques found in qualitative research. Meta-analysis is no substitute for a good literature review.

10

Evaluation and Policy Analysis

Policy analysis is defined as the use of any evaluative research to improve or legitimate the practical implications of a policy-oriented program. Program evaluation is done when the policy is fixed or unchangeable. Policy analysis is done when there's still a chance that the policy can be revised. A number of other terms are probably deserving of definition:

— *action research*: just another name for program evaluation of a highly practical nature

— *applied research*: a broad term meaning something practical is linked to something theoretical

— *continuous monitoring or audit*: determining accountability in activities related to inputs

— *cost-benefit analysis*: determining accountability in outputs related to inputs

— *evaluability assessment*: determining if a program or policy is capable of being researched

— *feasibility assessment*: determining if a program or policy can be formulated or implemented

— *impact analysis or evaluation*: finding statistically significant relationships using a systems model

— *needs assessment*: finding service delivery gaps or unmet needs to re-establish priorities

— *operations research*: another name for program evaluation using a systems model

— *organizational development*: research carried out to create change agents in the organization

— *process evaluation*: finding statistically significant relationships between activities and inputs

— *quality assurance*: ensuring standards for data collection appropriate for program objectives

— *quality circles*: creating employee teams that conduct research on organizational quality problems

— *quality control*: ensuring data utilized for decision making is appropriate

— *total quality management*: evaluation of core outputs from a consumer-driven point of view

Patton and many other good books, websites, and seminars on evaluation or grant and proposal writing will contain additional definitions. The basic principles and practices of evaluation are well-established, however. In criminal justice, unless you're willing to shop for sponsors in the private sector among charitable foundations, the source of most research funding is the National Institute of Justice.

NIJ is the research branch of the U.S. Department of Justice. It is totally unlike the old LEAA/LEEP (now NCJRS) in that discretionary block grants (enabling topics of your own choosing) are a thing of the past. Since 1984 and every year since, NIJ comes out with their Research Plan for the upcoming year. It usually sets 7-8 areas they want evaluative research done in.

These priorities represent a compromise between the personal preferences of the Attorney General and what NIJ senior staffers believe to be the most critical areas. There's almost always something available for research with drugs, domestic violence, victims, community crime prevention, sentencing, and in recent years, technology. Not much NIJ-sponsored research supports criminological research, and what little there is is eaten up by think tanks or well-organized academic research teams.

NIJ seems to favor proposals that involve randomized experimental designs and a clear indication that both academics and practitioners will be working closely together. Juvenile grants are handled by another agency, OJJDP (Office of Juvenile Justice and Delinquency Prevention), and most of the priorities there tend to heavily involve collaboration with lawyers or law-related education.

Systems Model Approach

To understand evaluative research, one must understand the systems model approach. Other words for this approach are theory-driven or criterion-driven. The basic idea is that any program, organization, or functional unit of society can be represented as an interrelated series of parts that work together in cybernetic or organic fashion. In fact, computer language is often used to describe the things an evaluator looks for, such as:

- *Inputs*: any rules, regulations, directives, manuals, or operating procedures, including costs, budgets, equipment purchases, number of authorized and allocated personnel
- *Activities*: anything that is done with the inputs (resources) such as number of cases processed, kinds of services provided, staffing patterns, use of human and capital resources

— *Events*: things that happen shortly before, after, or during the evaluation period such as Supreme Court decisions, changes in legislation, economic/political changes, natural disasters, etc.

— *Results*: specific consequences of activities or products produced, such as number of cases closed or cleared, productive work completed, or completed services provided

— *Outcomes*: general consequences or accomplishments in terms of goals related to social betterment such as crime rate declines, fear of crime reductions, deterrence, rehabilitation, etc.

— *Feedback*: any recycling or loop of information back into operations or inputs, such as consumer satisfaction surveys, expansion or restriction due to demand, profitability, etc.

In addition, evaluation research requires a fairly good grasp of administrative or management models, particularly those that have to do with planning, organizing, and control functions. At a minimum, the researcher should be familiar with the following generic model of all organizations:

MISSION

↓

GOALS

↓

OBJECTIVES

↓

BEHAVIOR

The mission is, of course, easily obtainable in the form of a mission statement or some declaration of strategic purpose. It's the one thing that the organization holds up to the outside world, or external environment, as it's connection to goals of social betterment.

Goals are those general purposes of the functional divisions of the organization. For example, to improve traffic flow, to deter crime, to solve cases, and to return stolen property are broadly-stated goals. They're the things that clientele or consumers of the agency relate to.

Objectives are specific, measurable outcomes related to goals, such as a 30% improvement in traffic flow, a 25% reduction in crime, or $500,000 in returned property. They are also usually time-specific, and are what employees most relate to.

Behavior is the ordinary productivity of employees. Accountability of behavior to objectives is the personnel function, and of behavior to goals or mission is oversight. Feedback loops normally exist between behavior and goals in most communication channels, however. Evaluators usually identify forces in the external environment (events), like demography, technology, economics, and politics, as well as who the clientele are of the organization (it's not the same as consumers), as well as the degree to which the organization is extracting power resources from its community vis-a-vis some competitive organization.

Steps of Program Evaluation

Program evaluations are often expected to involve some original research design, and sometimes what is called a triangulated strategy, which means 2-3 research designs in one (for example, a quantitative study, some qualitative interviews, and a secondary analysis of data collected from a previous program evaluation). The basis steps are the same as the scientific inference process:

— hypothesize;

— sample,

— design, and

— interpret.

The hypothesis step is crucial. The evaluator must dream up hypotheses that not only make sense for the kind of practical, agency-level data to be collected, but ones that are theoretically significant or related to issues in the field as evidenced from a review of the extant literature. Evaluators draw upon a wide range of disciplines, from anthropology to zoology. In Justice Studies, it's common to draw hypotheses having to do with offenses from the field of criminal justice and hypotheses having to do with offenders from the field of criminology.

Sampling is often not random since few organizations are willing to undergo experiments or deny treatments to some of their customers for the sake of research. Quasi-experiments or time-series may be the best that the evaluator can do. Sometimes, ANCOVA, or post-hoc statistical controls can be used as substitutes for experiments.

The design step usually involves replication of instruments, indexes, or scales used by previous researchers in studies of similar organizations. Occasionally, the evaluator will develop, pretest, and validate their own scale.

Interpretation results in the production of at least three documents: a lengthy evaluation report geared for a professional audience which contains the statistical methodology; a shorter report geared for laypeople which simplifies or summarizes the study; and an executive summary which is usually two or three pages in length and can also serve as a press release. In addition, evaluators often do interim and progress reports.

Steps of Policy Analysis

Policy analysis generally takes more time than program evaluation. Whereas all the above can be accomplished by a seasoned evaluator in six months or less, policy analysis may take a year or more. It may even take that long just to find out exactly when, how, and where the policy is articulated. A key operating assumption among policy analysts is that policy is never directly measurable. If it were a simple matter of looking up the statutory authority for the agency, there would be no reason for policy analysis, although it's common for policy analysts to at least pay homage to "policies enacted in law."

Policy analysis is most useful when you've got a large, troubled organization manifesting a Roshomon Effect (employees disagree or don't know the policies) and decoupled subenvironments. There's also usually some public concern about the morality or "goodness" of the organization, and policy analysis is not concerned with disinterested description, but with recommending something on the basis of moral argument. It's unfortunate that policy studies and policy analysis are typically limited to graduate school education. Learning the art and craft of policy analysis can be of enormous benefit to undergraduates, especially in Justice Studies. The basic steps of systematic policy analysis are as follows:

— *Problem Identification*: finding the public interests and issues involved

— *Criteria Selection*: determining what criteria to evaluate the organization on

— *System Assessment*: analysis of boundaries, feedback, and power dynamics

— *Strategies and Tactics*: examining decision-making and delivery mechanisms

— *Feasibility Assessment*: formulation and implementation analysis

A problem is defined as some predicted condition that will be unsatisfactory without intervention. They can stem from problems that everyone is already aware of, but in most cases, are derived the policy analyst's perception of what's appropriate for the organization.

This is sometimes called a constrained maximization approach because it involves reflection on the broader societal purpose (public interest) of the organization as well as what the top decision-makers are cognizant of. The analyst often derives a perception of the public interest from a literature review, or engages in what is called agenda building, which is similar to how sociologists approach a social problem or issue by analyzing the criminalization or medicalization of something. Intended and unintended functions of the organization as well as formal and informal agendas are looked at.

The selection of criteria depends on the public interests being served. It's time for some overdue examples, so let's take a typical code of ethics for an organization. Almost all of the verbiage in these can be reduced to the values of liberty, equality, and fraternity. The analyst would therefore try to construct formulas to measure liberty, equality, and fraternity in terms of the inputs, activities, and outcomes we became familiar with in our earlier discussion of program evaluation.

Actual mathematical formulas are constructed to measure abstract concepts. Much of the science behind it comes from the way economists measure opportunity cost. It makes more than a few people quantiphobic, Here explain a select few of the simplest ones:

— *Effectiveness*: Calculated by % gain scores toward defined objectives

- *Efficiency*: Calculated by dividing outcomes by inputs
- *Productivity*: Calculated by dividing # of outcomes by quality of activities
- *Equality*: Calculated by comparing the mean service delivery to a consumer who gets everything to a consumer who gets nothing
- *Equity*: Calculated by comparing the mean service delivery to the minimum allocation each social group should receive compared to zero allocation
- *Deterrence*: Calculated by multiplying # of crimes deterred by the average cost of crime
- *Incapacitation*: Calculated by multiplying the average of priors by the average period of incarceration
- *Rehabilitation*: Calculated by subtracting the recidivism rate from the velocity rate (number of priors after first arrest or while out on bail)

A system assessment in policy analysis usually involves creating a flowchart showing how outcomes and feedback are produced by the organization.

Here refers to whether or not there is an informal employee "culture" that accepts or rejects the policies inferred by the analyst. One of the assumptions of policy analysis is that practices do not make policy, but sometimes it seems like they do, so the analyst has to look into the goodness of fit, if you will, with the intentions of those practices and if the discrepant employees are what are called knowledgeables, or those people who are capable of thinking one step up to the abstract principles or interests behind policy. It may well be that the organization is fulfilling broader interests like health, well-being, or quality of life.

Systems, of course, also intimately involve boundary mechanisms, both externally to the environment and internally. It's the analyst's job to determine if these boundaries are open or closed, as this matters for the adaptive capacity of the organization and its readiness to accept change. The general rule is that permeability is healthy. Open organizations are more adaptive and changeable. Feedback loops are also open or closed, depending on the amount and use of information from outside consumers or clientele or internally from employees only. Many criminal justice agencies have criminal consumers, so it's customary to see terms like semi-permeable or semi-closed.

Strategies and tactics involve measuring the delivery mechanisms of the organization. In this regard, the analyst is concerned with informal and formal power structures. The powerless informal people will have their satisficing (settling for less) behavior measured. The powerful decision makers will have the degree to which they say (and they always do) they can improve with more time, money, and people measured. It's the job of the analyst to determine what are called the optimization levels for resource allocation.

11

Scaling and Indexing

Creating scales, indexes, or any measurement/assessment instrument that might be called a test is part of the research process that is concerned with calibration. In many ways, calibration is a quick and easy way to achieve precision and accuracy, which are, of course, important goals of measurement.

There are big difference between scaling and scoring a test, and since most readers are familiar with the typical multiple choice tests found in education, that's where we'll start. It's not uncommon for social sciences to draw upon the field of Education Statistics. You'll probably have to take such a course in graduate school if you plan to do any teaching.

Development of Test

A test is a series of questions designed to measure the nature and extent of individual differences. In the educational context, most people are familiar with the achievement-type test, which is designed to capture individual differences in knowledge. Screening process is recommended for obtaining the best pool of police applicants are

— screening-out

— screening-in

— lateral screening

— vertical screening

The multiple choice format is based on certain principles or rules. First of all, the sentence stem in the question should be short, clearly stated, and well-written. On October 31, 1998, Sam robbed the Acme Bank while wearing a Halloween mask and carrying a gun. While speeding from the crime scene, Sam lost control of his Jeep Cherokee and ran into a telephone pole.

When the police, who had previously received a bulletin about the bank robbery, arrived at the accident scene and saw the Halloween mask and bag of money in Sam's car, they immediately placed him under arrest for bank robbery, frisked him, and then asked him: "Where's the gun?" Sam replied that the gun was in his glove compartment. The police retrieved the gun, placed Sam in the patrol car, and drove him to police headquarters. As Sam was getting out of the squad car, he asked: "How many years am I going to have to do for the bank robbery?" Sam's lawyer has moved to suppress both statements, because Miranda warnings were not administered until after he was inside police headquarters.

The court should suppress: A. Sam's statement to the police about the location of his gun B. Sam's statement "How many years am I going to have to do for the bank robbery?" C. neither statement D. both statements. The answers in multiple choice format (the length depending upon instructor preference: A, B, C, D, E or A, B, C, D) should contain one and only one true and correct answer. That doesn't mean the answer has to the most clear, concise, comprehensive answer ever written; it just means that one response is completely true and correct.

Answers should also be short, clearly stated, and well-written. All the items other than the true and correct answer are called distracters. It's important to follow the principle that all distracters be plausible enough to sucker at least 2% of respondents into guessing at it. Poor, ridiculous, or "Mickey Mouse" distractors like "The police should let Sam go because bank robbery isn't all that bad" should be avoided.

Item analysis with our multiple choice achievement test example would involve looking at distracter patterns (the 2% rule), the difficulty level, and the discrimination index. To calculate the latter two, you need to sort all your completed tests in some rank order, from best to worse. Then, you take the top 27% of the best and the bottom 27% of the worst, and work out the following formulas.

Difficulty Index: # of people in best group who got item right + # of people in worst group who got item righttotal number of people in both groups

Discrimination Index: # of people in best group who got item right - # of people in worst group who got item right(.5) total number of people in both groups

The Difficulty Index is going to be a number from .00 to .99, and ideally, you want a number in the moderately difficult range (from .50 to .70). The Discrimination Index is going to be a number from -1.00 to +1.00, and ideally, you want a number in the twenties (from .20 to .29). Anything above that means you are favoring your brighter respondents.

A zero, near-zero, or below means that you are rewarding chance, or guessing, since four responses spell out to a 25% equal probability of getting it right, and the 27% best-worst dichotomy you made with this formula controls for this. There are tradeoffs between difficulty and discrimination, however. As difficulty goes up, discrimination approaches zero.

Scale Development

A scale is a cluster of items that taps into a unitary dimension or single domain of behavior, attitudes, or feelings. They are sometimes called composites, subtests, schedules, or inventories. Aptitude, attitude, interest, performance, and personality tests are all measuring instruments based on scales. A scale is always unidimensional, which means it has construct and content validity. A scale is always at the ordinal or interval level, but it's conventional for researchers to treat them as interval or higher. Scales are predictive of outcomes (like behavior, attitudes, or feelings) because they measure underlying traits (like introversion, patience, or verbal ability). It's probably an overstatement, but scales are primarily used to predict effects, as the following example shows:

A great many scales can be found in the literature or in handbooks, and beginning researchers are well-advised to borrow or use an established scale before attempting to create one of their own. However, most researchers are interested in breaking new ground, and have at least some hunch about what are variously called "tipping points", "the last straw", "going over the edge", or "snapping." It's this hardening, intensity, potency, or coming together of behavior, attitudes, and feelings that the researcher is calling a "trait" or something inside the person that is hopefully captured in scale construction. Scaling is all about quantifying the mysterious mental world of subjective experience.

There are four ways to construct scales:

— Thurstone scales

— Likert scales

— Guttman scaling

— Semantic differential

Thurstone scales were developed in 1929 for measuring a core attitude when you have multiple dimensions or concerns around that attitude. Take gun control, for instance. A person might have one part of their attitude relating to self-defense; another part of their attitude relating to constitutional rights; and still another part of their attitude relating to child safety. How do you determine which part of the attitude goes to the core of the matter? In

Thurstone scaling, the researcher would obtain a panel of judges (say 100 of them) and then dream up every conceivable question you can ask about gun control (say 100 questions). By administering that questionnaire to the panel, the researcher can analyze inter-item agreement among the judges, and then even use the discrimination index (explained above) to weed out what are called the nonhomogenous items. Scaling is all about homogeneity, a term sometimes used as synonymous with being unidimensional.

Likert scales were developed in 1932 as the familiar five-point bipolar response format most people are familiar with today. These scales always ask people to indicate how much they agree or disagree, approve or disapprove, believe to be true or false. There's really no wrong way to do a Likert scale, the most important thing being to at least have five response categories (for ordinal-treated-as-interval measurment).

The "don't know" is the second example is optional, and some people prefer not to use it since it's an odd response category. The examples showing "About 50/50", "Need more information", or "A bit of both" are preferable to use. You can increase the ends of the scale by adding "very" to create 7-point scales, which tends to reach the upper limits of reliability. It's best to use as wide a scale as possible since you can always collapse the responses into condensed categories later on for analysis purposes.

Guttman scaling was developed in the 1940s and is a technique of mixing questions up in the sequence they are asked so that respondents don't see that several questions are related. A lot of irrelevant questions surround the important questions. The scoring system is based on how closely they follow a pattern of ever-increasing hardened attitude toward some topic in the important questions. Let's take the example of attitude toward capital punishment:

1. Crime is a serious problem in the United States.
2. Police should be given more powers.
3. More criminals should be given the death penalty.
4. The U.S. ought to do something about drug exporting countries.
5. The military ought to be used to patrol our streets.
6. Inmates on death row ought to be executed quickly.
7. Most politicians are too soft on crime.
8. Lethal injection is too merciful for those who deserve it.
9. Crime is destroying the social fabric of our society.
10. They ought to jack up the voltage when they electrocute criminals.

In the above example, items #3, 6, 8, and 10 make up the scale for attitude toward capital punishment. Everything else is irrelevant. You should see how the relevant items lead progressively to a harder and harsher attitude. If most of the respondents you study (or the top 27% of them) hold fast to this hierarchical pattern, you've captured a very one dimensional aspect of your construct.

In addition, you can calculate something called the coefficient of reproducibility, which is simply 1 minus the number of breaks with the hardened response pattern divided by the total number of responses. Guttman scaling is very appealing, but it's not all that well-received by the scientific community. A variation is the Bogardus social distance scale, but it has properties of the semantic differential also.

The Semantic Differential is a technique developed in the 1950s to deal with emotions and feelings. It's based on the idea that people think dichotomously or in terms of polar opposites such as good-bad, right-wrong, strong-weak, etc. There are many varieties of the technique, the most popular one asking respondents to place their own slash mark along a line between adjectives. Let's take the example of a scale intending to measure feelings toward rap music as a cause of crime:

You can use the semantic differential with any adjectives you choose, and they don't even have to make sense. The point is to collect response patterns that you can analyze for scaling purposes. To quantify a semantic differential, all you do is overlay a Likert-type scale on top of it, and assume the endpoints are extremes such as "very bad" or "very good." You can also use a ruler and obtain precise numerical measurements. Throw out the items that don't correlate well with one another, and you've got a very precise and accurate scale.

Index Development

An index is a set of items (questions) that structures or focuses multiple yet distinctly related aspects of a dimension or domain of behavior, attitudes, or feelings into a single indicator or score. They are sometimes called composites, inventories, tests, or questionnaires. Like scales, they can measure aptitude, attitude, interest, performance, and personality, but the only kind of validity they have is convergent (hanging together), content, and face validity.

It is possible to use some statistical techniques (like factor analysis) to give them better construct validity (or factor weights), but it is a mistake to think of indexes as multidimensional (no such word exists) since even the most abstract constructs are assumed to have unidimensional characteristics. Indexes are usually at the ordinal, but mostly interval level. Indexes can be predictive of outcomes (again, using statistical techniques like regression), but they are designed mainly for exploring the relevant causes or underlying symptoms of traits (like criminality, psychopathy, or alcoholism).

Indexes are usually administered in the form of surveys or questionnaires. It's only at the time of report writing that you claim to have developed an index. You'll need an ideal response rate of 35% on your questionnaire, and at least a 5-point Likert scale for the response categories. There are a variety of ways to do surveys. Factor analysis, cluster analysis, or other advanced statistical techniques are typically used for item analysis of surveys.

Factor Analysis and Cluster Analysis

These are advanced methods of data analysis that require special training and proficiency at using computerized statistics programs like SPSS. Factor analysis can help develop an index, test the unidimensionality of a scale, assign weights (factor loadings) to items in an index, and statistically reduce a large number of indicators to a smaller set.

It works by a process known as ipsative scoring which places all the numbers in a variance-covariance matrix and then performs multiple iterations (repeats) on this matrix until the most statistically meaningful common denominators can be found. These meanings may or may not be theoretically significant. If you're lucky, only one factor, or common denominator will be produced. Ordinarily, factor analysis produces 4-5 such factors, and the researcher then has to justify discarding them in favor of the core set of items for their index or scale.

Cluster analysis is a similar technique, but more in keeping with the way reliability coefficients are produced. It involves iterative computer runs on your data matrix that continually resorts and reclassifies your groupings and categories into the most elegant mathematical matrix. The result is a tree and branch diagram which shows you which items are are most connected to the others. Both factor and cluster analysis are avoided by many researchers in favor of plain old fashioned looking at inter-item correlations.

Reliability and Item Analysis

The concept of reliability of measurement as used in social sciences (but not in industrial statistics or biomedical research). The term reliability used in industrial statistics denotes a function describing the probability of failure (as a function of time). In many areas of research, the precise measurement of hypothesized processes or variables (theoretical constructs) poses a challenge by itself. For example, in psychology, the precise measurement of personality variables or attitudes is usually a necessary first step before any theories of personality or attitudes can be considered.

In general, in all social sciences, unreliable measurements of people's beliefs or intentions will obviously hamper efforts to predict their behavior. The issue of precision of measurement will also come up in applied research, whenever variables are difficult to observe. For example, reliable measurement of employee performance is usually a difficult task; yet, it is obviously a necessary precursor to any performance-based compensation system.

In all of these cases, Reliability & Item Analysis may be used to construct reliable measurement scales, to improve existing scales, and to evaluate the reliability of scales already in use. Specifically, Reliability & Item Analysis will aid in the design and evaluation of sum scales, that is, scales that are made up of multiple individual measurements (e.g., different items, repeated measurements, different measurement devices, etc.). You can compute numerous statistics that allows you to build and evaluate scales following the so-called classical testing theory model.

The assessment of scale reliability is based on the correlations between the individual items or measurements that make up the scale, relative to the variances of the items. The classical testing theory model of scale construction has a long history, and there are many textbooks available on the subject.

Main Ideas of Assessment of Scale Reliability

Suppose we want to construct a questionnaire to measure people's prejudices against foreign- made cars. We could start out by generating a number of items such as: "Foreign cars lack personality," "Foreign cars all look the same," etc. We could then submit those questionnaire items to a group of subjects (for example, people who have never owned a foreign-made car). We could ask subjects to indicate their agreement with these statements on 9-point scales, anchored at 1=disagree and 9=agree.

True scores and error: Let us now consider more closely what we mean by precise measurement in this case. We hypothesize that there is such a thing (theoretical construct) as "prejudice against foreign cars," and that each item "taps" into this concept to some extent. Therefore, we may say that a subject's response to a particular item reflects two aspects: first, the response reflects the prejudice against foreign cars, and second, it will reflect some esoteric aspect of the respective question.

For example, consider the item "Foreign cars all look the same." A subject's agreement or disagreement with that statement will partially depend on his or her general prejudices, and partially on some other aspects of the question or person. For example, the subject may have a friend who just bought a very different looking foreign car.

Testing hypotheses about relationships between items and tests: To test specific hypotheses about the relationship between sets of items or different tests (e.g., whether two sets of items measure the same construct, analyze multi-trait, multi-method matrices, etc.) use Structural Equation Modeling (SEPATH).

Classical Testing Model

To summarize, each measurement (response to an item) reflects to some extent the true score for the intended concept (prejudice against foreign cars), and to some extent esoteric, random error. We can express this in an equation as:

$$X = \text{tau} + \text{error}$$

In this equation, X refers to the respective actual measurement, that is, subject's response to a particular item; tau is commonly used to refer to the true score, and error refers to the random error component in the measurement.

Reliability

A measurement is reliable if it reflects mostly true score, relative to the error. For example, an item such as "Red foreign cars are particularly ugly" would likely provide an unreliable measurement of prejudices against foreign-made cars. This is because there probably are ample individual differences concerning the likes and dislikes of colors. Thus, this item would "capture" not only a person's prejudice but also his or her color preference. Therefore, the proportion of true score (for prejudice) in subjects' response to that item would be relatively small.

Measures of reliability: From the above discussion, one can easily infer a measure or statistic to describe the reliability of an item or scale. Specifically, we may define an index of reliability in terms of the proportion of true score variability that is captured across subjects or respondents, relative to the total observed variability. In equation form, we can say:

$$\text{Reliability} = s2_{(\text{true score})} \,/\, s2_{(\text{total observed})}$$

Sum Scales

What will happen when we sum up several more or less reliable items designed to measure prejudice against foreign-made cars? Suppose the items were written so as to cover a wide range of possible prejudices against foreign-made cars. If the error component in subjects' responses to each question is truly random, then we may expect that the different components will cancel each other out across items. In slightly more technical terms, the expected value or mean of the error component across items will be zero. The true score component remains the same when summing across items. Therefore, the more items are added, the more true score (relative to the error score) will be reflected in the sum scale.

Number of items and reliability: Number of Items and Reliability is basic principle of test design. Namely, the more items there are in a scale designed to measure a particular concept, the more reliable will the measurement (sum scale) be. Perhaps a somewhat more practical example will further clarify this point. Suppose you want to measure the height of 10 persons, using only a crude stick as the measurement device.

Note that we are not interested in this example in the absolute correctness of measurement (i.e., in inches or centimeters), but rather in the ability to distinguish reliably between the 10 individuals in terms of their height. If you measure each person only once in terms of multiples of lengths of your crude measurement stick, the resultant measurement may not be very reliable. However, if you measure each person 100 times, and then take the average of those 100 measurements as the summary of the respective person's height, then you will be able to make very precise and reliable distinctions between people. Let us now look at some of the common statistics that are used to estimate the reliability of a sum scale.

Cronbach's Alpha

To return to the prejudice example, if there are several subjects who respond to our items, then we can compute the variance for each item, and the variance for the sum scale. The variance of the sum scale will be smaller than the sum of item variances if the items measure the same variability between subjects, that is, if they measure some true score. Technically, the variance of the sum of two items is equal to the sum of the two variances minus (two times) the covariance, that is, the amount of true score variance common to the two items.

We can estimate the proportion of true score variance that is captured by the items by comparing the sum of item variances with the variance of the sum scale. Specifically, we can compute:

$$a = (k/(k-1))^{*} [1- S_{(s2i)/s2sum}]$$

This is the formula for the most common index of reliability, namely, Cronbach's coefficient alpha (α). In this formula, the s_i**2's denote the variances for the k individual items; s_{sum}**2 denotes the variance for the sum of all items.

If there is no true score but only error in the items (which is esoteric and unique, and, therefore, uncorrelated across subjects), then the variance of the sum will be the same as the sum of variances of the individual items. Therefore, coefficient alpha will be equal to zero. If all items are perfectly reliable and measure the same thing (true score), then coefficient alpha is equal to 1. (Specifically, 1-Σ(s_i**2)/s_{sum}**2 will become equal to (k-1)/k; if we multiply this by k/(k-1) we obtain 1.)

Alternative terminology: Cronbach's alpha, when computed for binary (e.g., true/false) items, is identical to the so-called Kuder-Richardson-20 formula of reliability for sum scales. In either case, because the reliability is actually estimated from the consistency of all items in the sum scales, the reliability coefficient computed in this manner is also referred to as the internal-consistency reliability.

Split-Half Reliability

An alternative way of computing the reliability of a sum scale is to divide it in some random manner into two halves. If the sum scale is perfectly reliable, we would expect that the two halves are perfectly correlated (i.e., r = 1.0). Less than perfect reliability will lead to less than perfect correlations. We can estimate the reliability of the sum scale via the Spearman-Brown split half coefficient:

$$r_{sb} = 2r_{xy} /(1+r_{xy})$$

In this formula, rsb is the split-half reliability coefficient, and rxy represents the correlation between the two halves of the scale.

Correction for attenuation

Now consider some of the consequences of less than perfect reliability. Suppose we use our scale of prejudice against foreign-made cars to predict some other criterion, such as subsequent actual purchase of a car. If our scale correlates with such a criterion, it would raise our confidence in the validity of the scale, that is, that it really measures prejudices against foreign-made cars, and not something completely different. In actual test design, the validation of a scale is a lengthy process that requires the researcher to correlate the scale with various external criteria that, in theory, should be related to the concept that is supposedly being measured by the scale.

The random error portion of the scale is unlikely to correlate with some external criterion. Therefore, if the proportion of true score in a scale is only 60% (that is, the reliability is only .60), then the correlation between the scale and the criterion variable will be attenuated, that is, it will be smaller than the actual correlation of true scores. In fact, the validity of a scale is always limited by its reliability.

Given the reliability of the two measures in a correlation (i.e., the scale and the criterion variable), we can estimate the actual correlation of true scores in both measures. Put another way, we can correct the correlation for attenuation:

$$r_{xy,corrected} = r_{xy} \,/\, (r_{xx} * r_{yy})^{½}$$

In this formula, $r_{xy,corrected}$ stands for the corrected correlation coefficient, that is, it is the estimate of the correlation between the true scores in the two measures x and y. The term r_{xy} denotes the uncorrected correlation, and r_{xx} and ryy denote the reliability of measures (scales) *x* and *y*. You can compute the attenuation correction based on specific values, or based on actual raw data (in which case the reliabilities of the two measures are estimated from the data).

Designing a reliable scale

After the discussion so far, it should be clear that, the more reliable a scale, the better (e.g., more valid) the scale. As mentioned earlier, one way to make a sum scale more valid is by adding items. You can compute how many items would have to be added in order to achieve a particular reliability, or how reliable the scale would be if a certain number of items were added.

However, in practice, the number of items on a questionnaire is usually limited by various other factors (e.g., respondents get tired, overall space is limited, etc.). Let us return to our prejudice example, and outline the steps that one would generally follow in order to design the scale so that it will be reliable:

Generating items: The first step is to write the items. This is essentially a creative process where the researcher makes up as many items as possible that seem to relate to prejudices against foreign-made cars. In theory, one should "sample items" from the domain defined by the concept. In practice, for example in marketing research, focus groups are often utilized to illuminate as many aspects of the concept as possible.

For example, we could ask a small group of highly committed American car buyers to express their general thoughts and feelings about foreign-made cars. In educational and psychological testing, one commonly looks at other similar questionnaires at this stage of the scale design, again, in order to gain as wide a perspective on the concept as possible.

Choosing items of optimum difficulty: In the first draft of our prejudice questionnaire, we will include as many items as possible. We then administer this questionnaire to an initial sample of typical respondents, and examine the results for each item. First, we would look at various characteristics of the items, for example, in order to identify floor or ceiling effects.

If all respondents agree or disagree with an item, then it obviously does not help us discriminate between respondents, and thus, it is useless for the design of a reliable scale. In test construction, the proportion of respondents who agree or disagree with an item, or who answer a test item correctly, is often referred to as the item difficulty. In essence, we would look at the item means and standard deviations and eliminate those items that show extreme means, and zero or nearly zero variances.

Choosing internally consistent items: Remember that a reliable scale is made up of items that proportionately measure mostly true score; in our example, we would like to select items that measure mostly prejudice against foreign-made cars, and few esoteric aspects we consider random error.

Returning to Step 1: After deleting all items that are not consistent with the scale, we may not be left with enough items to make up an overall reliable scale (remember that, the fewer items, the less reliable the scale). In practice, one often goes through several rounds of generating items and eliminating items, until one arrives at a final set that makes up a reliable scale.

Tetrachoric correlations: In educational and psychological testing, it is common to use yes/no type items, that is, to prompt the respondent to answer either yes or no to a question. An alternative to the regular correlation coefficient in that case is the so-called tetrachoric correlation coefficient. Usually, the tetrachoric correlation coefficient is larger than the standard correlation coefficient, therefore, Nunally discourages the use of this coefficient for estimating reliabilities. However, it is a widely used statistic.

12

Ethics in Criminological Research

Ethics in research is hard to separate from the political, economic, administrative, and legal considerations. Most assuredly, there's a philosophical basis to research ethics, but instead, we'll focus on the practical considerations. A point to remember, however, is that there's no such thing as perfectly ethical research. In fact, all research is inherently unethical to some degree.

This is because you're using the most powerful tools science has to offer in getting at truth or some needed change, and with your results, somebody's going to be proven wrong or lose out in the power struggle. Research is all about power and sometimes creating inequalities where a placid consensus may have existed before. There's also no such thing as totally harmless research. Somebody, usually your subjects, is going to be harmed, either psychologically, socially, physically, or economically.

Their privacy is, and should be, invaded to get any useful information, and this is psychological harm. Socially and physically, you're harming them by taking up their time with your silly research, and economically, you're exploiting them by not paying them for their contribution. You, the researcher, will go on and become famous writing a book about them, but they will always remain lowly research subjects. Ethically, research is just a whole awkward and asymmetrical situation overall.

Let's consider the concept of "value-free" social science research. A lot of people advocate this as the sine quo non of research ethics, as if impartiality and objectivity were all there is to it. Actually, there are a number of models for the ethical purpose of research:

— *The Value-Free Model*: the idea here is that rigorous research will yield results that can be used for anyone's benefit, for good or evil, for better or worse, and that in the long run, good will win out over evil if researchers adhere to methodological rigor and consistency

— *The Social Problems Model*: the idea here is that research is problem solving, all about understanding the world we live in a little better so that we can modify it toward some greater good

— *The Marxist Model*: the idea here is that there are three kinds of research: trivial; that which aids the bourgeoisie (or haves); and Marxist research which aids the proletariat (the have-nots).

— *The Vulnerable Populations Model*: the idea here is that research ought to be used to uplift or empower those social groups who lack power in society, especially by qualitative research which gives them a "voice"

— *The Government Pawn Model*: the idea here is that research ought to be of use to government decision makers so that better public policy can be made

— *The Corporate Shill Model*: the idea here is that research should be used to promote the interests of wealthy, powerful individuals or corporations with researchers for sale in "think tanks"

There's also probably a Self-Imposed Morality Model where the researcher simply refuses to cave in to any pressures or ideology. Research is a lot like a thesis or dissertation in grad school; once the first draft is in the hands of your committee, it no longer is yours, but takes on a life of its own, reflecting the many interests of gatekeepers and stakeholders all around you.

Political Regulation of Research

Historically, governments have had to put serious restrictions on researchers. In fact, the origin of codes of research ethics can be traced to the Nuremberg Code, a list of rules established by a military tribunal on Nazi war crimes during World War II. The principles outlined in the Nuremberg Code include:

— Voluntary consent

— Avoidance of unnecessary suffering

— Avoidance of accidental death or disability

— Termination of research if harm is likely

— Experiments should be conducted by highly qualified people

— Results should be for the good of society and unattainable by any other means

The Nuremberg Code was followed by the 1948 U.N. Declaration of Human Rights and the 1964 Helsinki accord. All three documents are intended to forever ban anything like what Nazi doctors did – torture, maim, and murder – to captive subjects in concentration camps.

In 1971 (and revised in 1981), the U.S. government initiated guidelines for all federally funded research. Although some departments, like Justice, eventually developed their own guidelines, most federal agencies followed the lead of HEW (now HHS) because this list of rules could be applied generically to both medical and nonmedical research. The HEW GUIDELINES were:

— Subjects should be given a fair explanation of the purpose and procedures of the research

— Subjects should be given a description of any reasonable risks or discomforts expected

— Subjects should be told of any possible benefits to be obtained by participating

— Researchers should disclose any alternative procedures that might be advantageous to the subject

— Researchers should offer to answer any questions subjects may have during the research

— Subjects should be told they are free to withdraw and discontinue participation at any time

One of the outcomes of the HEW guidelines was the establishment of Institutional Review Boards (IRBs) at colleges and universities across America. IRBs regularly disapprove or delay research at most universities. At first, these institutions were seen as a hindrance on academic freedom by faculty researchers, but they came to be accepted, especially after 1981 when the revised HHS guidelines exempted most social science and criminal justice research from full review by creating a category of "expedited" review. Klockars and O'Connor boiled down the three basic principles governing most criminal justice research about this time:

— *Respect for persons*: the right to informed consent

— *Beneficence*: minimization of harm and maximization of benefits

— *Justice*: equitable distribution of benefits and burdens

Support for exempted and expedited research caught on in other social sciences, not just criminal justice. Current federal guidelines exempt from IRB review almost any surveys or interviews, as long as care is taken to ensure unique identifiers, or link files (matching subject's real names to a code number), are kept secret by the researcher, there is no risk of criminal or civil liability, and the research doesn't deal with sensitive issues, like unreported crime, drugs, sex, or alcohol.

Unobtrusive research is almost always exempt. The field of education enjoys more exemptions; anything related to variation on normal educational practices, such as curricula and instructional changes, is exempt. The field of psychology likewise has more freedom to experiment with perception, cognition, game theory, and test development, although the idea of manipulation of subjects is looked at closely by review boards. The point is you're not going to get a federal grant nowadays unless your research proposal has been approved by a local university's Institutional Review Board, and the best news you can hear from them is that your research is exempt or expedited.

Justice department grants have their own special rules. They pretty much adhere to HHS guidelines, but add concerns for embarrassment, criminal liability, and confidentiality. Embarrassment is regarded the same as harm and considered as how tactfully the researcher words the questions. "How many times have you beat your wife last month" might be considered an embarrassing question whereas "How many times did an instance of domestic violence erupt" would not be embarrassing.

This poses limitations on operationalization in much criminal justice research. Potential embarrassment is also a standard used in filmmaking if the researcher plans to take any video. Participants in NIJ-sponsored research are also supposed to be protected from criminal prosecution if they admit to anything during the research, but most researchers draw the line if they find out, for example, that one of their subjects plans to kill somebody. If the criminal justice researcher anticipates a dangerous situation arising from their research, they had better obtain a certificate of confidentiality from NIH and comply with NIJ provisions on privacy and confidentiality.

Filling out such forms activates a little-known "shield law" which protects the researcher from government prosecution for any liability or complicity in what their subjects do. It may also protect the researcher from any civil suits brought by survivors or family. It will not protect the researcher from libel or slander if the researcher goes public, and it will not protect the researcher from disclosing information to a grand jury or in response to a court order.

Researchers and their subjects are not a privileged relationship at law. They can be compelled to reveal their sources. A catch-22 therefore exists. If the researcher is ordered by a grand jury or court to reveal what they know, say a research subject who told them "I'm going to kill that [insert libelous remark here] ", the researcher cannot be held liable for the killing but can be held liable for libel and slander. Often, it's the university the researcher is affiliated with that has to pick up the tab for legal costs and libel/slander judgments, and it's extremely important that the researcher is a tenured professor with academic freedom rights.

The problem of political regulation of research is even more aggravated when one tries to do cross-national research. Something as simple as public opinion surveys are banned in most countries, including most of Asia, eastern Europe, and Africa. In a number of nations, sociology and anything called "sociological" is banned as subversive. Anything called "criminology" is banned in most of Latin America, especially if the research has got anything to do with drugs, police brutality, corruption, or juvenile sexual behavior.

There's an organization called COSSA (Consortium of Social Science Associations) which is working to remedy the problem of "forbidden" research topics in foreign nations, but they have a long way to go. As with all grantsmanship, a couple of phone calls and the right connections go a long way. The CIA and NSA have long hired researchers to do national security work for them under the guise of academic research. Sometimes, researchers are duped into doing this kind of work without knowing who's really funding their research. Most ethical researchers will not accept such assignments, or if they find out, terminate their research, but many accept and stay on because military and national security grants are lucrative.

Under the Export Control Act of 1985, researchers who break the blanket rule not to disclose their secret funding or tick off a national security agency in some way can be forever barred from traveling overseas for scholarly or academic purposes. Even in the U.S., often government-sponsored research cannot be released to the public until a political appointee approves the final release document.

Bad Social Science Research

There's no shortage of bad research examples, but we'll limit ourselves to five of the most well-known cases in social science. It's customary to note that these cases are frequently cited in the literature, talked about in classrooms, and even have movies or documentaries about them.

The Cyril Burt Affair: Cyril Burt was a famous British criminologist in the early 20th century who wanted to prove Lombroso and Goddard right that there were "born criminals" and that they were feeble-minded or had low intelligence. You'll sometimes find him mentioned in criminology textbooks as the "father of twin studies." After it was discovered that Goddard faked his photographs to make the eye sockets of Irish immigrants look more deeply receded, it was also discovered that Burt faked his data and published phony tables of numbers showing such people had low IQs. The affair is memorable as a lasting tribute to the "publish or perish" environment in academics, where professors, like Burt, need to get promoted by rushing into print with research results. Mistakes like the Burt Affair are similar to other scams, frauds, plagiarisms, and coverups that still go on in research today, most notably in anthropology.

Tearoom Trade: was the name of a book published by a sociologist named Laud Humphreys in 1970 who posed as a "watchqueen" in public restrooms to observe homosexual behavior. After every liaison where an old man would seduce some "chicken hawk" with money for an oral sex experience, Humphreys would jot down the license plate number of each old man's vehicle. Then, he had a friend in the police department trace the addresses. He would then visit the old men at home and pressure them into giving him an interview. The case stands as a classic example of invasion of privacy.

Obedience To Authority: was the name of a book by psychologist Stanley Milgram in 1974 who wanted to see how far people would be willing to turn up the dial, if ordered to do so, on a machine that pretended to give electrical shocks to people in the next room. You'd be surprised how many people were willing to go all the way, even though some broke down in tears after hearing fake screams coming from the other room. The experiment stands as testament to doing psychological harm.

Tuskegee Syphilis Study: was conducted from 1932 to 1974 and involved the withholding of penicillin from Black male sharecroppers so the government could find out the long term effects of syphilis. Similar experiments went on with the U.S. military involving nerve gas and nuclear radiation. The CIA also performed bizarre mind control experiments involving LSD, ESP, hypnosis, and surgery. The moral of all this is not to conduct secret testing on unsuspecting subjects.

Zimbardo's Prison Simulation: was a study by psychologist Philip Zimbardo in 1972 that took Stanford University undergrads and made some of them guards and some of them prisoners in a mock underground dungeon for a planned two week stay. The experiment had to be cancelled after six days because by then, the student-guards became quite sadistic, really getting into their roles. The prisoners were also becoming quite mental. The experiment tells a story about psychological harm and informed consent, since the subjects didn't know what they were getting into.

Economic Regulation of Research

Economic regulation is the issue of who sponsors your research as well as how much money you get. Be advised that with grants, you never get the full amount you ask for, but you can sometimes persist and get more than what is first offered. A lot of grants will not let you hire assistants, especially student assistants. Most grants will not pay for first-class travel, and travel is one of the first things cut, so you might have to ride Greyhound if you have to go anywhere.

Many grants today require a matching amount from your own employer, sometimes in cash and other times in kind. Expect to run out of money before your research is finished, and don't be surprised if your employer eats up some of your grant money. Your employer will also set up administrative procedures to doll the money out to you on a requisition basis.

The quickest and easiest way to experience economic exploitation in research is to go work for one of those so-called "think tanks" in criminal justice. There's hundreds of them, all non-profits, and all with names like the National Institute for something-or-other. They are usually located around the Washington D.C. beltway, and they constantly keep their eye out for possible RFPs (Requests for Proposals) by following the Federal Register (proceedings of Congress), so they have a firsthand shot with grant proposals at-the-ready long before any announcement is made to the public.

Contract research, or think tank studies, vary greatly in quality, lack peer review, and are short on solid evidence but long on suggestions. Think tank agencies, whether Institutes or Foundations, all have an agenda of their own to publicize, and publicity is what drives the research. The audience is not the scientific community, but politicians (who get free copies of reports) and any other consumer who stumbles upon their website and order page for their publications (although some reports are free, usually after a year or two of shelf life for not selling well).

The ideology is apparent in most of these research reports as the researcher is forced to advocate some policy recommendation that fits or meshes well with the avowed aims of the think tank. The media also tends to treat many think tank reports as gospel, and some think tank researchers obtain quite a bit of media notoriety. Unfortunately, much better research never gets published or ends up in a data repository like the ICPSR (Inter-University Consortium for Political and Social Research).

It's the ethical duty of a researcher to get their results published somewhere. This is called dissemination of your research, and it requires that you find the most appropriate and scholarly outlet that you can. Most major universities have their own in-house publishing company you should look at as a last resort. The exception to this is law school journals which you should look at as your first choice. In criminal justice, it's possible to rank the journals in terms of their scholarly reputation. As a researcher, you should get a handle on which journals are ranked more highly than others.

An economic problem exists with doing campus-based research. Say, you're interested in doing a study on campus crime, however, the university administration thinks that the image of the school as well as its economic fortune (in terms of admissions) will be affected by your study. You'll find the same sort of economic rationale behind city administrators who attempt to block your study on the community gang problem because the city doesn't want to admit they have a gang problem.

Don't succumb to the temptation of paying your subjects for participating in research. Always use volunteers. Research is, after all, a gift of knowledge that your subjects freely give to you and you're supposed to freely give to the world. There are three ways, and three ways only, to encourage participation ethically:

— *Anonymity*: promise and keep your promises of anonymity. After identifying your sampling frame, try to forget about taking names or any other unique identifiers. Reassure people that you won't go to the media. Fill them in on what journal outlet you have planned. Threaten to destroy your documents if they're worried about your response to being subpoenaed.

— *Confidentiality*: this is what you should promise if you can't keep anonymity. In other words, use confidentiality if you can't guarantee anonymity. This is one of the basic rules of research. It requires that you guarantee that no one will be individually identifiable in any way by you, that all your tables, reports, and publications will only discuss findings in the aggregate.

— *Informed Consent*: Be honest and fair with your subjects. Tell them everything they want to know about your research. Be aware of any hidden power differentials that might be pressuring them to participate. For example, if you're a teacher or authority figure of any kind, and your subjects consist of your students or people in a status reporting to you in some other way, then reflect upon the possibility that they're participating for the possibility of unintended side benefits.

Vulnerable Populations

Laws often exist, depending upon jurisdiction, to safeguard the rights of various people in research activities. These populations include, but are not limited to inmates, crime-stricken communities, children, pregnant women, and those with disabilities. There are strict limits on the types of research that can be conducted on inmates or prisoners.

Under no circumstances is a researcher allowed to even suggest that by participating in research, it will reflect favorably on their record when they go up for parole or early release. The same sort of rule applies to criminal suspects and defendants; you can't promise them any leniency of any kind, or even that you will tell the judge about it, or anything like that.

You can say that your research might benefit the whole class of inmates, prisoners, suspects, or defendants as a group. And, you can say that you're experimenting with something innovative or creative involving improvement of the justice system. NIJ's CFR 45 also requires that, with inmates, the study present no more than the common inconveniences common to the situation of a typical prisoner. You cannot, for example, design an experiment, involving conditions of confinement below the minimum standard of living at the jail or prison.

With certain crime-stricken communities, you might have what are called equity concerns, which means that if one neighborhood is receiving the benefit of some new service, another neighborhood is not receiving the benefit. Most Justice majors are familiar with the Kansas City Patrol Experiment in which certain sectors got intensive police protection and other sectors got none.

You can't do these things anymore according to most laws. If you must, and cannot get the project approved as an exemplary experiment (requiring federal approval), then consider what is called a crossover design, which switches neighborhoods around in place, from control group to experimental group, so that everyone eventually receives the benefit. You don't have to keep collecting data if you don't want to, since you're only doing it as part of an equity component of your project.

Children as research subjects present special problems, and it is best to avoid using them unless you cannot. First of all, a legal guardian or parent must grant you written permission to conduct your research. Secondly, any authorities in charge of any grounds or locations which involve your research must also give their permission for you to conduct your research. It's probably not possible to list the complete network of agencies involved with most juveniles, but suffice it to say that, as researcher, you're going to need to at least touch base with a lot of people. It's best to ask permission from the juveniles too.

Pregnant women, those with disabilities, and those who are incompetent in some way (such as mental retardation) are generally not allowed to participate in research. This tends to limit research on forensic populations, such as serial killers, for example, but it depend upon how psychotic they are. The FBI profilers can get away with it because they argue the good outweighs the harm, but the average researcher is probably going to need the permission and/or supervision of clinical psychologist, at least. Several psychometric (and personality) testing instruments are not to be administered by anyone other than a competent psychometrician or psychologist. It's best to get medical advice when using such subjects.

Informed Consent

A full blown consent statement would contain the following:

- A brief description of the purpose and procedure of the research, including the expected duration
- A statement of any risks, discomforts, or inconveniences associated with participation
- A guarantee of anonymity or at least confidentiality, and an explanation of both
- The identification, affiliation, and sponsorship of the research as well as contact information
- A statement that participation is completely voluntary and can be terminated at any time without penalty
- A statement of any alternative procedures that may be used
- A statement of any benefits to the class of subjects involved
- An offer to provide a free copy of a summary of the findings

Responsible Conduct in Research

Misconduct in Science

Beyond honest errors and errors caused through negligence are a third category of errors: those that involve deception. Making up data or results (fabrication), changing or misreporting data or results (falsification), and using the ideas or words of another person without giving appropriate credit (plagiarism)- all strike at the heart of the values on which science is based. These acts of scientific misconduct not only undermine progress but the entire set of values on which the scientific ènterprise rests. Anyone who engages in any of these practices is putting his or her scientific career at risk. Even infractions that may seem minor at the time can end up being severely punished.

The ethical transgressions discussed in earlier sections-such as misallocation of credit or errors arising from negligence-are matters that generally remain internal to the scientific community. Usually they are dealt with locally through the mechanisms of peer review, administrative action, and the system of appointments and evaluations in the research environment. But misconduct in science is unlikely to remain internal to the scientific community. Its consequences are too extreme: it can harm individuals outside of science, it squanders public funds, and it attracts the attention of those who would seek to criticize science. As a result, federal agencies, Congress, the media, and the courts can all get involved.

Within the scientific community, the effects of misconduct-in terms of lost time, forfeited recognition to others, and feelings of personal betrayal-can be devastating. Individuals, institutions, and even entire research fields can suffer grievous setbacks from instances of fabrication, falsification, or plagiarism even if they are only tangentially associated with the case.

When individuals have been accused of scientific misconduct in the past, the institutions responsible for responding to those accusations have taken a number of different approaches. In general, the most successful responses are those that clearly separate a preliminary investigation to gather information from a subsequent adjudication to judge guilt or innocence and issue sanctions if necessary. During the adjudication stage, the individual accused of misconduct has the right to various due process protections, such as reviewing the evidence gathered during the investigation and cross- examining witnesses.

In addition to falsification, fabrication, and plagiarism, other ethical transgressions directly associated with research can cause serious harm to individuals and institutions. Examples include cover-ups of misconduct in science, reprisals against whistleblowers, malicious allegations of misconduct in science, and violations of due process in handling complaints of misconduct in science. Policymakers and scientists have not decided whether such actions should be considered misconduct in science-and therefore subject to the same procedures and sanctions as falsification, fabrication, and plagiarism-or whether they should be investigated and adjudicated through different channels.

Regulations adopted by the National Science Foundation and the Public Health Service define misconduct to include "other serious deviations from accepted research practices," in addition to falsification, fabrication, and plagiarism, leaving open the possibility that other actions could be considered misconduct in science. The problem with such language is that it could allow a scientist to be accused of misconduct for using novel or unorthodox research methods, even though such methods are sometimes needed to proceed in science.

Federal officials respond by saying that this language is needed to prosecute ethical breaches that do not strictly fall into the categories of falsification, fabrication, or plagiarism and that no scientist has been accused of misconduct on the basis of using unorthodox research methods. This area of science policy is still evolving.

Another category of behaviors-including sexual or other forms of harassment, misuse of funds, gross negligence in a person's professional activities, tampering with the experiments of others or with instrumentation, and violations of government research regulations-are not necessarily associated with scientific conduct. Institutions need to discourage and respond to such behaviors. But these behaviors are subject to generally applicable legal and social penalties and should be dealt with using the same procedures that would be applied to anyone.

13

Development of Psycholegal Research

The plethora of applications of psychology to law can be differentiated in terms of what has been defined as: (a) 'psychology in law'; (b) 'psychology and law'; and (c) 'psychology of law'. Psychology in law refers to specific applications of psychology within law: such as the reliability of eyewitness testimony, mental state of the defendant,and a parent's suitability for child custody in a divorce case.

Psychology and law is used by Blackburn to denote, for example, psycholegal research into offenders, lawyers, magistrates, judges and jurors. Finally, psychology of law is used to refer to psychological research into such issues as to why people obey/disobey certain laws, moral development, and public perceptions and attitudes towards various penal sanctions.

As far as the term forensic psychology is concerned, Blackburn argues convincingly it should only be used to denote the 'direct provision of psychological information to the courts, that is, to psychology in the courts'.While there is no generally acceptable definition of 'legal psychology', the following one put forward by Ogloff is sufficiently broad and parsimonious, as he maintains, to reduce some of the confusion that surrounds this field: 'Legal psychology is the scientific study of the effects of law on people; and the effect people have on the law.

Legal psychology also includes the application of the study and practice of psychology to legal institutions and people who come into contact with the law.' Psycholegal research involves applying psychology's methodologies and knowledge to studying jurisprudence, substantive law, legal processes and law breaking. Research into, and the practice of, legal psychology has a long tradition exemplified since the beginning of the twentieth century by the work of such pioneersas Binet, Gross, Jung, Münsterberg and Wertheimer.

In fact, Münsterberg has been called 'the father of applied psychology'. Ogloff mentions Cattell's article in Science which was concerned with how accurately one could recall information; Freud's lectures to judges in Vienna on the merits of psychology for law in establishing facts; Watson's view that judges could utilise psychological findings and Paynter's and Burt's research into trademark and trade name infringements which was presented in court; Hutchins and Slesinger's published work on psychology and evidence law and, finally, the Russian psychologist Luria's work on the affect in newly arrested criminals, before being interrogated by police, in order to differentiate the guilty from the innocent.

Regarding publications in law and psychology, the following appeared in the early part of the twentieth century: Brown's Legal Psychology: Psychology Applied to the Trial of Cases, to Crime and its Treatment, and to Mental States and Processes; Hutchins and Slesinger's article on 'legal psychology' in the Psychological Review; McCarty's Psychology for the Lawyer and Cairns' Law and Social Sciences. The psycholegal field has been expanding at an impressive rate since the mid 1960s, especially in

North America, since the late 1970s in the UK and in Australia since the early 1980s.

In fact, on both sides of the Atlantic, research and teaching in legal psychology has grown enormously since the mid 1970s. More recently, the field of psychology and law has also been expanding in Europe, especially in the Netherlands, Germany and Spain. Since the 1960s psychology and law has evolved into a single applied discipline and an often-cited example of success in applied psychology. Ogloff maintains that, 'Despite its long history, though, the legal psychology movement has had limited impact on the law, and until recently, it was focused primarily in North America'.

Haney points to psycholegal researchers having tackled some very crucial questions in society and, inter alia, been instrumental in improving the ways eyewitnesses are interviewed by law-enforcement personnel; the adoption of a more critical approach to the issue of forensic hypnosis evidence in the courts; psychologists contributing to improving the legal status and rights of children; and, finally, generally making jury selection fairer. Furthermore, the impact of legal psychology has not just been one way. Despite the early publications in legal psychology mentioned above, and while most lawyers would be familiar with forensic psychology, traditionally dominated by psychiatrists, it was not until the 1960s that lawyers in the United States came to acknowledge and appreciate psychology's contribution to their work.

Since the 1970s a significant number of psycholegal textbooks have appeared in the United States,in England,and some have been written by legal psychologists on continental Europe. In addition, following Tapp's first review of psychology and law in the Annual Review of Psychology, relevant journals have been published, such as Law and Human Behavior which was first published in 1977 as the official publication of the American Psychology-Law Society (APLS) and is nowadays the journal of the American Psychological Association's Division of Psychology and Law.

Other journals are: Behavioural Sciences and the Law; Expert Evidence; Law and Psychology Review; Criminal Behaviour and Mental Health. New psycholegal journals continue to be published. The first issue of Psychology, Crime and Law was published in 1994 and those of Legal and Criminological Psychology and Psychology, Public Policy, and Law in 1996 in the UK and the United States respectively. Despite the fact that in the UK lawyers and psychologists have been rather less ready than their American colleagues to 'jump into each other's arms', the push by prison psychologists and increasing interest in the field had gathered enough momentum by 1977 for the British Psychological Society to establish a Division of Criminological and Legal Psychology.

By the early 1980s empirical contributions by legal psychologists at Aberdeen University added to the momentum. Annual conferences at the Oxford Centre formed the basis for Farrington et al.'s Psychology, Law and Legal Processes and Lloyd-Bostock's Psychology In Legal Contexts: Applications and Limitations, and these 'established a European focus for collaboration between the two disciplines, attracting scholars from many different countries' and paved the way for the more recent annual European Association of Psychology and Law (EAPL) Conferences.

These two publications, together with Clifford and Bull's The Psychology of Person Identification and other British works published in the 1980s and early 1990s, have established psychology and law as a field in its own right in Britain, despite the fact that in 1983 the Social Science Research Council, under a Conservative government, ceased funding conferences for lawyers and psychologists. Following a suggestion made at the EAPL conference in Siena, Italy, in 1996 by Professor David Carson of Southampton University, a very successful conference indeed was held at Trinity College, Dublin, jointly organised by APLS and EAPL.

The conference was attended by over 600 delegates from twenty-seven countries, and produced two excellent books, namely Psychology in the Courts: International Advances in Knowledge by Roesch et al. and Violent Sexual Offenders by Farrington et al.. Psychological associations outside the UK also set up relevant divisions, for example, in the United States in 1981 and in Germany in 1984. In 1981 the American Psychological Association founded Psychology and Law as its forty-first Division. A significant development in the United States was the inclusion in 1994 of law and psychology in the Annual Survey of American Law. Besides a spate of international conferences on legal psychology that have been held in the UK and on continental Europe, there now exist both undergraduate and post-graduate programs in legal psychology. Finally, a number of universities on both sides of the Atlantic have recognised the importance of legal psychology by dedicating chairs to the subject in psychology departments and law schools. It must not be forgotten, however, that while, by the beginning of the 1980s, one-quarter of graduate programs in the United States offered at least one course and a number had begun to offer forensic minors and/or PhD/JD programs, few psychology departments offered courses in psychology and law prior to 1973.

Bridging the Gap Between Psychology and Law

The development of sociological jurisprudence, with its emphasis on studying the social contexts that give rise to and are influenced by law, posed a challenge to the 'black-letter' approach to studying law which was based on the English common law and had been the linchpin of the legal system in North America. Sociological jurisprudence provided conditions within law that were favourable to the development of legal psychology, as did subsequent movements in law such as 'legal realism'.

In his book, On The Witness Stand, Münsterberg was critical of the legal profession in the United States for not appreciating the relevance of psychology to its work. However, Münsterberg was overselling psychology and his claims were not taken seriously by the legal profession. In addition, according to Cairns, there was opposition from within the discipline of psychology by such scholars as Professor Edward Titchener of Cornell University, who maintained that psychologists should not seek to apply their findings but should confine themselves to conducting pure and scientific research.

Not surprisingly, therefore, 'the initial foray into law and psychology...did not generate enough momentum to sustain itself'. The rather unfortunate legacy left by Ebbinghaus and his black-box approach to experimental memory research - best exemplified by his use of nonsense syllables - contributed to the state of knowledge in psychology at the time and was one significant factor that negated the success of Münsterberg's attempt.

Fortunately, the dominance of the black-box paradigm in experimental psychology came to an end with the publication in 1967 of Neisser's futuristic Cognitive Psychology book. In the ensuing six decades, whilst behaviourism (on the one hand) and the experimental psychologists' practice (on the other) of treating as 'separate and separable' perception, memory, thinking, problem solving and language permeated and limited psychological research greatly, the early interest in psycholegal research fizzled out. As Ogloff points out, the continuing development of legal psychology after the 1930s was not only prevented by forces within psychology but, also, by a 'conservative backlash in law which limited the progressive scholars in the field ... The demise of legal realism had a chilling effect on legal psychology ...'.

Ogloff lists the following possible lessons to be learned, and to avoid, from the demise of legal psychology after 1930: a small number of people working and publishing in law; lack of training programmes for students; no identi- fiable outlet for psycholegal research; that those supporting the psychological status quo did not look favourably upon psycholegal research and, finally, the fact that legal psychologists were not formally organised. By the late 1960s, as psychology matured as a discipline and, amongst other developments, social psychology blossomed in the United States, the experimental method came to be applied to problems not traditionally the concern of psychologists.

Psychologists began turning their attention to understanding deception and its detection, jury decision-making, the accuracy of eyewitness testimony and sentencing decision-making as human processes. Most of the early psycholegal researchers with a strong interest in social psychology focused on juries in criminal cases, those with an affinity to clinical psychology concerned themselves with the insanity defence, while cognitive psychologists examined eyewitness testimony. These same areas continue to be of interest to psycholegal researchers today, but the questions being asked are more intricate and the methods used to answer them are more sophisticated.

More recently, Ogloff, like Carson and Bull, has urged legal psychologists to broaden their research interests to include more areas of law, including: administrative law, antitrust, civil procedure, corporate law, environmental law, patent law, and family law. The somewhat narrow focus of psycholegal research caused enough concern to Saks for him to remind such researchers that 'the law does not live by eyewitness testimony alone' and for Diamond to urge them 'to explore underrepresented areas of the legal landscape'. It is comforting for psychologists to know that, with the genèral growth and maturity of their discipline, major industrialised society has come to realise the wide-ranging benefits of psychology.

Why, then, has it taken so long for the field of psychology and law to develop when, as some authors would argue,psychologists and lawyers do have a lot of common ground? Both disciplines focus on the individual. Yarmey wrote that 'both psychology and the courts are concerned with predicting, explaining and controlling behaviour', while according to Saks and Hastie: 'Every law and every institution is based on assumptions about human nature and the manner in which human behaviour is determined'. Achieving 'justice' is the concern of law and lawyers, while the search for scientific truth is the concern of psychologists.

Crombag argues that law may be considered a branch of applied psychology because the law mainly comprises a system of rules for the control of human social behaviour. Listing law as a component of psychology, however convincing the arguments put forward for it might be, is not a suggestion that will endear psycholegal researchers to lawyers. A more realistic position to adopt than that of Crombag's is that 'to the extent that every law has as its purpose the control or regulation of human behavior, every law is ripe for psychological study'.

While the law relies on assumptions about human behaviour and psychologists concern themselves with understanding and predicting behaviour, both psychology and law accept that human behaviour is not random. More specifically, research in psychology relates to various aspects of law in practice. As in other countries, the legal profession in Australia, justifiably, perhaps, has been rather slow to recognise the relevance of psychology to its work.

Compared to law, psychology is, chronologically speaking, entering its adulthood and, given a number of important differences between the two disciplines, it comes as no surprise to be told that there is tension, and conflict between the two disciplines that persists. Bridging the gap between the two disciplines on both sides of the Atlantic, in Australia, New Zealand and Canada, as well as, for example, in Spain and Italy has not been easy. In fact, there is a long way to go before the remaining ambivalence about psychology's contribution to academic and practising lawyers and ethical issues of such a function will be resolved.

Admittedly, 'Different psychologists have different ideas about what psychology should be about' and 'Law, like happiness, poverty and good music, is different things to different people'. The simple fact is that there are significant differences in approach between psychology and law. This point is well-illustrated by eight issues which, according to Haney are a source of conflict between the two disciplines, namely:

— The law stresses conservatism; psychology stresses creativity.

— The law is authoritative; psychology is empirical.

— The law relies on adversarial process; psychology relies on experimentation.

— The law is prescriptive; psychology is descriptive.

— The law is idiographic; psychology is nomothetic.

— The law emphasizes certainty; psychology is probabilistic.

— The law is reactive; psychology is proactive.

— The law is operational; psychology is academic.

It can be seen that the two disciplines operate with different models of man. The law, whether civil or criminal, generally emphasises individual responsibility in contrast to the tendency by a number of psychological theories to highlight 'unconscious and uncontrollable forces operating to determine aspects of individuals' behaviour'. In addition, 'The psychologists' information is inherently statistical, the legal system's task is clinical and diagnostic'.

As Clifford has put it: 'the two disciplines appear to diverge at the level of value, basic premises, their models, their approaches, their criteria of explanation and their methods'. In a submission to the Australian Science and Technology Council in the context of its investigation into the role of the social sciences and the humanities in the contribution of science and technology to economic development it is stated that: 'Psychology discovers, describes and explains human experience and behaviour through the logic and method of science.

Psychological research and application is based in a logical, empirical and analytical approach, and that approach is brought to bear on an exceptionally wide range of issues.'On the other hand, 'Tradition is important to lawyers' and, as Farrington et al. put it, law 'is a practical art, a system of rules, a means of social control, concerned with the solving of practical problems'. Furthermore: 'The law is based on common-sense psychology which has its own model of man, its own criteria ... its own values.

Common-sense explanation in the law is supported by the fact that workable legal processes have evolved under constant close scrutiny over many centuries. It is in this sense "proven". But this is quite different from explanation in terms of psychological theory backed by empirical evidence of statistically significant relationships'.

Finally, whereas the image of human beings projected by American social psychologists is that of the 'nice person', the law, and especially the criminal law, is characterised by a more cynical view of human nature and this view tends to be adopted by those who work within and for the legal system.

Psycholegal researchers (for example, in eyewitness testimony) have utilised a variety of research methods including incident studies, field studies, archival studies and single case studies. Many psychologists rely a great deal on the experimental method, including field experiments, to test predictions and formulate theories that predict behaviour and are sceptical of lawyers' reliance on common-sense generalisations about human behaviour based on armchair speculation, however ratified by conceptual analysis.

A feature that unifies a lot of psychological research is its preference for subjecting assertions to systematic empirical research and, where possible, testing them experimentally. This will often involve randomly allocating persons to different conditions who, at the time, are normally not told the aim of the experiment. Clifford provides an excellent account of contemporary psychology's premises and methods. Many psychologists who favour experimental simulation tend not to also consider the issue of values in psychological and psycholegal research in general, and in particular whether psychologists can indeed avoid value judgements by demonstrating the 'facts'.

Theoretical models of man espoused by experimental psychologists have involved man as a black box, a telephone switchboard and, more recently, man as a computer. These models, which are different from the lawyer's notion of 'free will', have been rejected by cognitive psychologists because they do not take into account man as a thinking, feeling, believing totality, as someone who interacts with the environment in a dynamic way.

For many a psychologist, a great deal of information processing is done without people being aware of it; the lawyer, on the other hand, operates a model of man as a free, conscious being who controls his/her actions and is responsible for them. What the law, based on a lot of judicial pronouncements, regards as 'beyond reasonable doubt' is rather different from the psychologist's conclusion that an outcome is significant at a 5 per cent level of statistical significance.

One interesting aspect of this, for example, is the lawyer's reluctance to quantify how likely guilt must appear to be before one can say that such doubt as exists is not reasonable. The lawyer in court is often only interested in a 'yes' or 'no' answer to a question asked of a psychologist who is appearing as an expert witness, while, at best, the psychologist may only feel comfortable with a 'maybe' response. It should be noted, however, that the answers of interest to a practising lawyer might vary according to whether it is examination in chief or cross-examination.

In the former, the lawyer is interested in a story, whereas in the latter, the lawyer is interested in questions that require a 'yes' or 'no' answer. Also, lawyers look at the individual case they have to deal with and highlight how it differs from the stereotype; they try hard to show in court that one cannot generalise, whereas psychologists talk about the probability of someone being different from the aggregate. In addition to significant differences between psychology and law, there is the fact that the approaches of various branches of psychology differ in the degree to which they are based on what might be called scientific experiments.

Furthermore, some psychologists have cast doubt on the practical utility of findings from controlled laboratory experiments that reduce jury decision-making, for example, to a few psychology undergraduates reading a paragraph-long, sketchy description of a criminal case and making individual decisions on a rating scale about the appropriate sanction to be imposed on the defendant.

Rabbitt pointed out that 90 per cent of the studies quoted in standard textbooks on the psychology of memory then available only tested recognition or recall of nonsense three-letter syllables. More recently, Konecni and Ebbesen have argued that: 'It is dangerous and bordering on the irresponsible to draw conclusions and make recommendations to the legal system on the basis of simulations which examine effects independently of their real-world contexts'.

More recent research on the jury includes protocol analyses, in-depth interviews with jurors after they have rendered verdicts in real cases, elaborate simulations involving videotaped trials and juror respondents, and even randomised field experiments.

Similarly, eyewitness testimony researchers have been making increasingly greater use of staged events and non-psychology students as subjects, as well as utilising archival data. King has also criticised legal psychologists' strong reliance on the experimental method, arguing that there is a tendency to exaggerate its importance; that treating legal factors as 'things' and applying to them experimental techniques and statistical methods gives rise to at least four problems, namely, inaccessibility, external validity, generalisability and completeness.

King has also argued that exclusive reliance on experimental simulation also encourages legal psychologists to focus on inter-individual behaviours without taking into account the social context to which they belong; that Karl Popper's refutability has been shown by philosophers of science to be a questionable criterion for defining whether a theory is scientific.

Furthermore, King contends that the real reasons for legal psychologists' continued use of the experimental method as the prime or sole method for studying legal issues is: (a) a belief by psychologists that using the experimental method enables them to claim they are being 'scientific' in carrying out their research; (b) a need felt by psychologists for recognition and acceptability; and (c) a belief by psychologists that they are more likely to be accepted and recognised as 'experts' if they are seen to be 'scientific'. Finally, neo-Marxist critics of the use of the experimental method 'see the failure to pay attention to the context of social behaviour as a political act perpetrated by psychologists in order to obscure the true form and content of social interaction'.

King has advocated a shift 'away from the restrictive and self-aggrandising notions of what constitutes "scientific" research which have tended to serve as a starting point for much of what passes for legal psychology'. No doubt many psychologists would disagree both with Wexler's picture of them as involved in a political conspiracy informed by a particular ideology and with King's push to get them to use the experimental method less in favour of ethnomethodology as their preferred methaod of enquiry.

Highlighting the dangers inherent in studying eyewitness testimony under rather artificial conditions in the laboratory, Clifford and Bull reminded their readers that such research could lead psychologists to advance knowledge that is, in fact, the reverse of the truth, as in the case of the influence of physiological arousal on recall accuracy. A theory of recall, or any other psychological theory for that matter, arrived at on the basis of grossly inadequate research could hardly be expected to be taken seriously by lawyers.

According to Hermann and Gruneberg, in the 1990s memory researchers no longer presumed that a laboratory procedure would or would not extrapolate to the real world because the ecological validity issue in memory research had largely been solved. Hermann and Gruneberg proposed that: 'It is time now to move beyond the ecological validity issue...to the next logically appropriate issue - applied research'.

14

Politics of Criminological Research

Criminological research is a political endeavour in two senses. Firstly, the political context inevitably shapes, to varying extents, all stages of the research process because criminologists are researching a social problem, which politicians seek to explain and control. Secondly, criminological researchers inevitably become embroiled in micro-political processes because research often seeks to understand the standpoints of different, sometimes opposing, groups.

Attempts to periodize the development of criminological theory are superficially attractive. Such simplification is inherent in the abundance of texts that outline the range of criminological perspectives. These texts tend to introduce the dominant perspective at a particular point in time, note how it was subjected to intense criticism by an emerging perspective, report its decline and then move on to discuss the new perspective which they now treat as the dominant one.

The pattern continues. The best texts note that adopting this structure is a pedagogic device, and attempt to convey some sense of the complexities that lie beneath the development of criminological theory. For instance, noting that seemingly 'new' perspectives often draw upon the influences of earlier ones. Bottoms distinguishes between five approaches to criminology: classicism, natural-science positivism, active-subject socially-oriented criminologies, active subject individually-oriented criminologies and political-activist criminologies.

For Bottoms, politicalactivist criminologies include Marxist-oriented criminologies, feminist criminologies and the theoretical movement known as 'left-realism'. Gaining dominance within British criminology since 1970, these perspectives have been somewhat openly political.

The combination of political activism and theorizing challenges traditional conceptions of the relationship between theory and research. As Bottoms suggests, the legacy of positivism has left criminology suspicious about political engagement for fear that their research may be perceived as unscientific. Political-activist criminology makes explicit that criminological theory and research are inseparable from the political landscape. However, there is a danger that political goals can override the pursuit of knowledge.

One of the key elements of Marxism is that all social phenomena, including crime, can be explained in terms of each society's economic relations. In capitalist society, the private ownership of the means of production allows the bourgeoisie to exploit the proletariat, and thus crime can be seen as part of the struggle in which the economically powerless proletariat attempt to cope with the exploitation and poverty imposed on them.

Bonger was the first to apply Marxist principles to crime but the Marxist tradition had little impact on criminology until the 1970s. At that time, a growing number of criminologists offered Marxist-inspired analyses of the problem of crime. They also went further to suggest that the solution to the crime problem lies in revolution, bringing about major social, economic and political change. Other criminologists were reluctant to adopt a pure form of Marxism, and instead attempted to fuse elements of interactionism with the fundamentals of Marxism. The result was the publication of The New Criminology by Taylor et al.. With the benefit of hindsight, this text is widely cited as the genesis of critical criminology.

Taylor et al. endeavoured to develop a criminological theoretical framework and to endorse a variety of radical politics through their insistence that a society based on principles of socialist diversity and tolerance would be free of crime. By the mid-1970s criminology was highly politicized. A growing concern with the process of criminalization provided the backdrop for critical criminologists to explore the ways in which power associated with the capitalist state asserts itself in relation to crime. The influence of Marx was joined by that of Foucault and Gramsci.

In simple terms, critical criminology seeks to explore the ways in which the variables of class, ethnicity and gender are played out in relation to crime and criminal justice. The concern of critical criminologists is not only with discriminatory practices but the ways in which structural inequalities are perpetuated. For instance, critical criminologists seek to understand the ways in which state practices seek to marginalize, and consequently criminalize, certain groups. The influence of feminism is apparent in critical criminological work.

The second wave of the women's movement in the late 1960s and early 1970s introduced a new dimension to criminological debates. It began by noting the misrepresentation, or more commonly neglect, of women in criminological theory, and attempted to redress the balance by focusing their attention on women as victims, offenders and criminal justice professionals. An important dimension to their work is the blurring of the boundary between theory and practice.

Feminist criminologists have been active in campaigning for law reform, changes to criminal justice policy and providing a range of support services for female victims of crime. In the mid-1980s, Left realism emerged in the UK as a response to both the utopianism of earlier Marxist-inspired criminologies and the punitive and exclusionary character of right realist policies in the US. Left realism still claimed to be radical in its criminology but combined this with a commitment to offer effective solutions to the crime problem. Rather than seeking to challenge the state, criminologists on the political left now sought to work with the state as part of an attempt to take crime seriously.

Shaping Criminological Research

Researchers working in any of the following organizations may conduct criminological research:

— higher education institutions;

— central government departments, sometimes in dedicated research units;

— criminal justice organizations, particularly large police forces and probation areas;

— private sector research organizations, for example, National Centre for Social Research; and

— voluntary sector organizations, for example National Association for Care and Resettlement of Offenders.

Criminological research may also be carried out by practitioners working in the criminal justice sphere. Reiner terms this group 'inside insiders'. Research may be done as part of a postgraduate degree or as part of a programme of work. Criminal justice professionals are also eligible to apply for a small number of awards including the Cropwood programme of short-term fellowship awards and the Police Research Award Scheme.

The growth of practitioner research is not peculiar to criminology, and there is a growing literature on the subject. There are multiple sources of funding available to criminological researchers. The organization which employs the researcher will determine the sources of funding they are eligible to compete for, and consequently the type of research that they can undertake. The main types of funders are listed in Table 1 below.

Table 1. Funding available for criminological research

Type of funder	Key funders
Government departments	Home Office; Youth Justice Board; Lord Chancellor's Department
Research councils (funded by Government)	Economic and Social Research Council
Charitable foundations	Joseph Rowntree Foundation; Nuffield Foundation; Leverhulme Trust
Local multi-agency partnerships	Crime and disorder partnerships; drug actions teams; youth offending teams
Criminal justice agencies	Police forces; probation areas; prisons

It might be helpful for readers to be familiar with the diverse sources of funding received to conduct criminological research. The CVs of many criminologists will also have an eclectic mix of funding sources. Here elaborate on the main types of funding for criminological research below, focusing on their research priorities and the procedures for obtaining research funding.

Government Funding

A major source of government funding for criminological research is the Home Office. The Home Office funds research in different ways. It has a dedicated research unit, the Home Office Research Development and Statistics directorate (HORDS) but also issues contracts to external research organizations. HORDS has appeared in different guises but dates back to 1956. It has always been a major locus of criminological research but has not always enjoyed an easy relationship with politicians.

The Conservative governments of 1979-90 were deeply phobic about criminological research. Michael Howard carefully scrutinized research during his term as Home Secretary and his junior minister went as far as proposing closure of the research section of the Home Office. Even before that date Home Office research was shifting towards an 'administrative criminology' agenda. This term, coined by Jock Young in the 1980s, refers to criminological research which abandons the search for the causes of crime and focuses its efforts on strategies and policies to prevent and deter crime.

The inclusion of the word 'planning' to create the Home Office Research and Planning Unit (HORPU) in 1981 Funding available for criminological research was more than symbolic. As Maguire notes, the Home Office moved towards a position where funding decisions were almost exclusively driven by narrow short-term policy concerns, and where the research questions, methods and timescale were ever more tightly established in advance by civil servants. This has the effect of losing sight of the broader academic debates, and runs the risk of neglecting more fruitful and innovative ideas.

Increased Home Office control over the research agenda has been described as the inevitable corollary of the party politicisationof law and order. When the Labour government came to power in 1997 they seemed committed to the information economy and were willing to invest substantial sums of money to develop it. In April 1999, the Crime Reduction Programme was launched. It ran for three years, with an overall budget of £250 million.

The programme comprised a series of diverse initiatives, dealing with a wide range of offences and every aspect of the criminal justice process. The aim of the programme was to establish what works in reducing crime as part of a commitment to evidence-based policy and practice. As a result, funding was made available for independent evaluation, always leading to the collection of quantitative data. Described by Morgan as 'the largest programme of criminological research ever undertaken in the United Kingdom', criminological researchers were divided in their response to the increased funding. Some sought to avoid involvement, suggesting that the work was theoretically impoverished and too closely allied to the interests of the state.

Others welcomed the opportunity to have some degree of involvement with the development of crime policy but were streetwise enough to recognize the political nature of the work. No doubt others were more pragmatic and opportunistic, unable to resist the large sums of money on offer. Research opportunities under the Crime Reduction Programme were only offered in response to invitation to tender. The majority of Home Office funding is allocated in this way, and concerns about the process have been aired elsewhere. Sometimes tenders are issued to a shortlist of applicants who have been requested previously to submit an expression of interest.

Typically researchers are sent a detailed document which is fairly prescriptive about the work to be undertaken. A further example is the Innovative Research Challenge Programme. This takes the form of an open competition, and its aims are described in the HORDS business plan 2001-02 as to enhance 'contact with the wider research community and building on its contribution to Home Office aims, but also to ensure that RDS research retains a long-term focus'.

Policy-oriented research can be innovative and intellectually challenging. It is possible to produce both a concise report devoted to answering the research questions asked by the funder, and to use the knowledge required to produce publications for an academic audience.

Research Council Funding

Criminological research comes largely under the remit of Economic and Social Research Council (ESRC). The ESRC was established in 1965 by Royal Charter as an independent organization. However, its £92 million budget for both research and postgraduate training comes mainly from the Government. In the 1990s, thematic priorities were developed in order to focus research on scientific priorities. There are seven in total, and criminological research can be related to all of them.

However, the two most important thematic priorities in relation to criminological research are 'Governance and Citizenship' and 'Social Stability and Exclusion'. They provide a focus for some, but not all, ESRC research activities. These include provision of funds for centres, programmes and grants. Since 1990, two programmes have been directly related to crime and 'Crime and Social Order'. In addition, funding has been made available for two research networks on pathways into and out of crime. Although the ESRC is widely regarded by the criminological community as the most prestigious source of funding, its strategies for allocating funds have been contested.

The ESRC make explicit their commitment to funding 'blue-skies' or curiosity-driven research alongside applied and strategic research. However, the incorporation of users' needs into various aspects of the research process has caused concern. The oft-perceived shift to only funding applied research and the subsequent loss of rigour are the most common causes of disquiet. Users in this context include industry, charities, universities, local authorities and other public bodies, government departments and independent policy bodies. Users are involved in a wide range of practices including setting thematic priorities for funding, evaluating research and shaping programmes.

Charitable Foundations

There are a number of charitable foundations that are willing to fund criminological research, although none of them have crime as their exclusive focus. In the UK, the major players are the Leverhulme Trust, the Nuffield Foundation and the Joseph Rowntree Foundation. The Leverhulme Trust has an annual budget of £25 million, and places emphasis on allowing applicants to choose the topic they wish to research. This form of responsive support is open to researchers from all disciplines.

In contrast, the Joseph Rowntree Foundation focuses solely on social policy research, and the £7 million budget funds both ongoing and timelimited research programmes. The Nuffield Foundation runs 14 different grant programmes including an 'open door' one, and gave out £6. 4 million in the form of research grants in 2002. While the programmes run by the Joseph Rowntree Foundation and Nuffield Foundation do not concentrate solely on aspects of crime and criminal justice, they do offer opportunities for research in areas of interest to criminologists including programmes, for example the Joseph Rowntree Foundation Drug and Alcohol Research Programme and the Nuffield Foundation's programmes on child protection and access to justice. Does who pays the piper call the tune?

Having described the various sources of funding available to criminological researchers. Research agendas are created by funders who have their own preferences for both the research topics and research approaches they wish to support. This applies to all three major sources of funding outlined above. The research programmes which emerge are the end product of a series of interactions between groups.

For government departments such as the Home Office, the key players are ministers, civil servants and HORSD. For research councils such as the ESRC, research priorities and programmes are developed by Council, which includes representatives from academia, business and the public sector. For charitable bodies, the trustees are influential in determining the research they are able to fund.

All these players will have to work within the parameters of their organization's role, and in the case of charitable trusts the original wishes of the benefactor. The extent to which funding bodies influence the actual conduct of research varies considerably. Those who enter in a 'customer-contract' relationship with the Home Office experience the greatest level of interest. This can take many forms including the submission of regular progress report and steering group meetings. Critics might interpret them as compromising the independent nature of the research that has been commissioned.

A more balanced view is to recognize the need to be cautious when public money is being invested in research, and to appreciate the support that can be offered, even if the level of involvement feels intrusive at times. Other funding bodies may not operate in the same way but do not give researchers a free rein. They may, for instance, require changes to be made to the research design and to be notified if the research differs from that laid out in the proposal. Even those university researchers whose research is unfunded are not free from the political agendas of government. The context in which they work is highly significant. Since 1989 a research assessment exercise has taken place periodically.

The stated purpose of this exercise 'is to enable the higher education funding bodies to distribute public funds for research selectively on the basis of quality', and one of the criteria on which decisions are made is the amount of external research funding received.

Politics of Postgraduate Research

Postgraduate students, if they have any funding at all, are likely to be in receipt of studentships from their own academic institution or from the ESRC. Postgraduate students still need to work within the broad parameters of ESRC funding but these researchers are likely to enjoy academic freedom to a far greater extent than their supervisors. This may only be appreciated after the event.

One of us has explored elsewhere how the political context can still be important for postgraduate researchers. Reflecting on doctoral research on prisons and bail hostels for women at a time of increasingly punitive responses to offenders, made the following comment.

> Although not financially sponsored by the state (both of us were awarded university studentships), our research was inevitably influenced by ... [the] political context in various ways. Explicitly,we were dependent upon the state for access to the criminal justice agencies we wanted to research. Implicitly, the political context impacted upon our relationships in 'the field'.

Drew attention to the relatively powerless position that postgraduates occupy within academic institutions even though they count considerably towards the rating their department receives in the Research Assessment Exercise. Retaining their academic freedom is one of the challenges postgraduates face. This became apparent at a session one of us (Wincup) ran on 'managing your supervisor' at the

2002 British Society of Criminology Conference. It was rather dispiriting, although not unexpected, to hear students suggesting that their supervisor had 'written' their thesis for them by driving the research in a direction most suited to their theoretical concerns.

Micro-politics of Criminological Research

As Downes and Morgan argue, the micro-politics of law and order are articulated in a wide range of settings in both the public and private sphere through the generation of talk about crime and how best to solve it. This influences research but also provides data for analysis. Described by Delamont as a 'manifesto on values and methods', his starting point is that neutrality is a myth shattered by the reality that personal and political sympathies inform research. This does not mean that the goal of research is the pursuit of political goals.

Instead, it challenges the aim of positivists and naturalists to strive as far as possible to limit the influences of values on the research process. Qualitative research has little in common with positivist principles but qualitative researchers have been proponents of naturalism. This perspective attempts to study the social world in its 'natural state', undisturbed by the researcher, and offer a detailed description of some aspect of social life ('to tell it how it is'). This perspective has been subjected to criticism by qualitative researchers.

The focus of Becker's essay was on research with deviant groups, chosen because researchers who focus on this group frequently have to answer to the charge that siding with deviant groups leads to distortion and bias. Becker suggests that a 'hierarchy of credibility' operates in deviancy research (and in other areas such as education), and credibility and the right to be heard are distributed differentially throughout the hierarchy.

Researchers interested in deviant groups concentrate on those whose voices are normally unheard, and hence challenge what Becker terms the 'established status order'.

According to Becker, accusations of bias are levelled only at researchers who focus on deviants rather those concerned with criminal justice professionals. For Becker, researchers always have to take sides, and their challenge is to ensure that unavoidable sympathies with our research participants do not render our work invalid. Becker's essay received criticism shortly after it was published by Gouldner who insisted that value-neutrality was possible and desirable.

Remarkably, over 35 years after its publication, Becker's essay continues to be revisited by social researchers. In her article on prisons research, Liebling argues that 'it is possible to take more than one side seriously, to find merit in more than one perspective, and to do this without causing outrage on the side of officials or prisoners. She does note, however, that this is a precarious business and risks encountering the wrath of criminologists who are sceptical of any attempt to understand officialdom. For Liebling, taking more than one side seriously does not lead to impartiality, and is therefore not a form of closet positivism.

Instead, attempts to synthesize different or competing perspectives within the prison world at the analysis stage help to sharpen our focus, and consequently this is a valuable analytic task. For many criminological researchers, regardless of whether they adopt Becker's position, they find themselves in the precarious position of trying to keep everyone happy. This is particularly true for those conducting research within criminal justice agencies who have to strive to avoid alienating opposing groups.

For example, Carter's study of the occupational socialization of prison officers involved forging positive relationships with staff and prisoners within the organizational hierarchy. The groups have the potential to be mutually antagonistic, leading him to describe the research process as a 'nerve-racking experience and a difficult road to walk for the researcher' . For Carter, the researcher has to be seen to be everyone's friend, attempting to understand their different points of view and appearing not to favour any one group or individual.

Publication and Dissemination Politics

There are numerous ways in which criminologists can publish their findings. Journal articles, research monographs, book chapters and research reports continue to have the greatest kudos in academic circles. The demands of the Research Assessment Exercise in the UK have placed particular importance on the production of peer-reviewed articles.

There are, of course, other opportunities to publish work. Potential outlets include practitioner journals, professional magazines, newspapers (particularly broadsheets), political magazines and journals produced by voluntary sector organizations. Technological developments have increased opportunities further, and it is now possible to find criminological research reported on websites and in electronic journals. Academic criminologists have yet to experiment with theatrical scripts as a means of conveying their research findings. They have been employed by other qualitative researchers, and this reminds us that dissemination does not have to be confined to the written word.

Submission of a research report of some kind is a requirement of all funders of criminological research. What happens next varies but all require a final report, which may be sent to academics with specialist expertise in the area to review. This happens for Home Office funded research, and the draft is also scrutinized by HORDS researchers and by policy-makers in different areas of the Home Office and in other government departments. Researchers are then asked to respond to the comments, and sometimes this process is repeated. It would be unfair to suggest that this practice is unhelpful.

Receiving constructive comments on a draft often leads to a more polished report, even if the feedback is a little painful to read at first. Similarly, observations from policy-makers can produce a more user-friendly, policy-relevant publication. However, the whole process can also be frustrating, not least because it can lead to immoderate delays. It can also produce contradictory feedback and suggested changes to the research design, which are of little use once the data have been collected.

Until the final report has been accepted, researchers working on Home Office projects need to ask permission to publish findings. A 'publish and be damned' attitude is unwise if researchers seek to receive future government funding, not least because researchers are expressively forbidden in their legal contracts to make public any findings prior to the publication of the final report without permission. At the extreme, state funded research may be subjected to censorship. Drawing on his considerable experience as a Home Office researcher (now working in a university), Mair reveals that he felt his work was never subjected to censorship. Anticipating his critics, he is keen to defend himself against the charge that his work was self-censored through gradual acceptance of repressive practices.

However, he does concede that he felt under indirect pressure to produce the 'right' results from his study of electronic monitoring. This illustrates that political pressures may not be explicit but form part of the social milieu in which the researcher works. There are, however, some examples of censorship. Here present two examples, which might be described as infamous. The first is Baldwin and McConville's Home Office funded study on the outcome of jury trials in Birmingham Crown Court. This was conducted in the mid-1970s. Drawing on the data gathered from over 100 interviews with defendants, they found repeated evidence of plea-bargaining. Since little had been written on the topic in the UK, the researchers hoped to publish a book in the area.

The reaction to the findings has been presented in-depth elsewhere. A confidential draft of the report was leaked to the media. The controversy caused led the Senate of the Bar to contact the Home Secretary urging him to discourage publication. The university put in place an inquiry after being warned by the Home Secretary about possible implications should the book be published. The book was eventually published in 1977.

The same year, Cohen and Taylor published an account of their attempts to publish research on long-term imprisonment, going as far as to suggest that their research was 'sabotaged' by the Home Office. The study employed qualitative methodology, an approach for which they receive a great deal of critical comment, and focused on how prisoners talked about their experiences of coping with lengthy custodial sentences. Despite their protests that the study was 'not particularly radical' and constituted an important piece of independent sociological inquiry, they found themselves 'trapped in a complex web of social and political restrictions'.

They note that official bodies such as the Home Office are able to exercise a high degree of control of research through five forces which they term as the 'centralization of power', 'legalisation of secrecy', 'standardization of research', 'mystifying the decision structure' and 'appealing to the public interest'. Ultimately these forces led to the decision to abandon the research rather than collude with the Home Office agenda.

Even if research is not funded by the state, publishing research findings can have political consequences. Whyte notes that presenting a paper on the findings of his critical criminological research on the oil industry to an industrial audience led to an abrupt end to his access to the Health and Safety Executive Offshore Safety Division. Hoyle shares her experience of publishing a book based on her PhD on policing domestic violence. She experienced extensive media publicity because of her unwillingness to support right-wing feminist calls for blanket arrest and prosecution policies and custodial sentences for all convicted abusers. For Hoyle, the criticisms stemmed from her failure to support political orthodoxy on domestic violence.

Making use of Criminological Research

The relationship between research and policy had been subjected to ongoing academic debate by social scientists, often leading to the establishment of typologies of the different forms the relationship can take. Of course research need not always have a direct recompense in this way. Travers argues that research might be done 'entirely for its own sake!'. In contrast, King implies that it is not sufficient for research to attempt to address challenging intellectual questions. Instead, researchers should aim to have at least some modest impact on society. This may not be immediate. As Hughes notes, research may have a long-term influence on both the policy and political process. Criminological research over time has the potential to challenge political discourses on law and order through generating debate.

One study alone is unlikely to change policy but a coherent and cumulative body of knowledge on a criminological issue might have an impact. This body of knowledge might consist of what has been termed 'basic' (concerned with producing theory) and 'applied' research. Criminologists are understandably impatient. There are plentiful examples of missed opportunities to influence policy, and criminologists must accept some of the blame for this. In a paper on young adult offenders and alcohol, Parker argues that British criminologists are ill-equipped to respond to, or moderate the power of, the law and order discourse.

For Parker, the dominant law and order discourse is 'alcohol plus young men equals violent crime'. British criminologists have largely retreated from qualitative, ethnographic communitybased studies of subculture and deviant lifestyles. Hence, there is a lack of authoritative explanations available to challenge the simplistic, blaming style of political discourse. There are also copious instances of developing policies which run counter to research findings. Frequently cited in this respect is the insistence by Michael Howard, when he was Home Secretary in 1993, that 'prison works' despite the wealth of research findings which suggested the contrary. This was his rationalization for pursuing a highly punitive approach to offending.

The National Audit Office (NAO) published a report in April 2003 suggesting that the gulf between academics and policy-makers means that much of the £1. 4 billion the government spends on research each year is wasted. To be clear, the report entitled Getting the Evidence: Using Research in Policy-Making focused on research commissioned by the Department of International Development, Office of the Deputy Prime Minister, and the Department for Environment, Food and Rural Affairs.

University academics are the most common recipients of these research contracts. Only a minority of these research budgets are likely to be concerned with areas of criminological interest. Nonetheless, it is worth considering their findings in more detail because the issues raised are likely to resonate with criminological researchers and policy-makers concerned with crime and criminal justice. Indeed similar arguments are advanced by Mair.

Some of the difficulties raised are practical ones, and included poor understanding of research results by policy-makers, inadequate communication of the research results by researchers, and too little being done to propagate findings. These can be resolved by developing research training courses for policy-makers, furthering the report writing skills of researchers, and enhanced dissemination activities.

The latter requires increased funding, exploration of more imaginative forms of dissemination to reach the widest audience possible, and clarification of whether the researcher or the funder is responsible for disseminating research findings. Bridging the gap between academics and policy-makers is more challenging. The NAO reported that the grasp of policy questions by researchers was inadequate but are careful to avoid blaming researchers.

15

Problems of Criminological Research

Domestic violence is not just a frequent crime, it is also costly-not only in terms of the injuries suffered by the parties involved but also in terms of shattered families. What to do about this major social problem, then, is an important policy question. One thing the police could do would be to respond to incidents of domestic violence in such a way that the offender would be less likely to be violent in the future. That is, proper police response could possibly prevent some acts of domestic violence. But what is the proper police response?

In 1981, the Police Foundation and the Minneapolis Police Department began an experiment to determine whether arresting accused spouse abusers on the spot would deter future offending incidents. In responding to police calls for service in misdemeanor domestic cases, the responding officer randomly assigned the case to be resolved by either arresting or not arresting the suspect on the scene. The experimental treatment, then, was whether the suspect was arrested, and the researchers wanted to know whether arrest was better than not arresting the suspect in reducing recidivism (subsequent assaults against the same victim). The study's results, which were widely publicized, indicated that arrest did have a deterrent effect.

Partly as a result of the reported results of this experiment, the percentage of urban police departments that made arrest the preferred response to complaints of domestic violence rose from 10% in 1984 to 90% in 1988. Six other cities then hosted studies like the Minneapolis experiment, but the results were not always so clear-cut as in the original study. In some cities (and for some people), arrest did seem to prevent future incidents of domestic assault; in other cities, it seemed only to make matters worse, contributing to additional assaults; and in still other cities, arrest seemed to have no discernable effect.

After these replications of the original Minneapolis experiment, people wondered, "Just what is the effect of arrest in reducing domestic violence cases, and how should the police respond to such cases?" The answer was not clear. The Minneapolis Domestic Violence Experiment, the studies modeled after it, and the related controversies provide many examples for a systematic overview of the social research process. The first concern in criminological research (indeed in any research) is deciding what to study. That is, how does one go about selecting an issue, problem, or question to address with research?

In criminology, as in any other science, theory plays an important role as a basis for formulating research questions and later understanding the larger implications of one's research results. Another motivation for research is one's personal interests. There is nothing wrong with researching those issues that you find fascinating or interesting.

Criminological Research Questions

A criminological research question is a question about

some aspect of crime or criminals that you seek to answer through the collection and analysis of firsthand, verifiable, empirical data. The types of questions that can be asked are virtually limitless. For example, "Are children who are violent when young more likely than nonviolent children to use violence as adults?" "Does the race of the victim who is killed influence whether someone is sentenced to death rather than life imprisonment?" "Why do some kinds of neighborhoods have more crime than others? Is it due to the kinds of people who live there or characteristics of the neighborhood itself?" "Does community policing reduce the crime rate?" "Has the U.S. government's war on drugs done anything to reduce the use of illegal drugs?"

So many research questions are possible in criminology that it is more of a challenge to specify what does not qualify as a social research question than to specify what does. But that doesn't mean it is easy to specify a research question. In fact, formulating a good research question can be surprisingly difficult. We can break the process into three stages: identifying one or more questions for study, refining the questions, and then evaluating the questions.

Identifying the Questions

Formulating a research question is often an intensely personal process in addition to being a scientific or professional one. Research questions may emerge from your "personal troubles," as C. Wright Mills put it, or your personal experiences. These troubles or experiences could range from how you felt when you were picked up by the police and perhaps arrested when you were a teenager for something you did not do, to the awareness you may have that crime is not randomly distributed within a city but that there seem to be "good" or safe parts of town and "bad" or unsafe areas.

You may find yourself asking questions such as "Do the police sometimes make things worse for people when they arrest them-worse in the sense that they are more likely to commit crime in the future?" or "Does victimization change a person's trust in others?" or "Does involvement in crime vary by one's age, social class, gender, or racial/ethnic group?" Can you think of other possible research questions that flow from your own experiences in the world? The experience of others is another fruitful source of research questions.

Knowing a relative who was abused by a spouse, seeing a TV special about violence, or reading a gang member's autobiography can stimulate questions about general criminological processes. Can you draft a research question based on a relative's experiences, a TV show, or a book? Other researchers may also pose interesting questions for you to study. Most research articles end with some suggestions for additional research that highlight unresolved issues. For example, Lawrence Sherman and Douglas Smith, with their colleagues, concluded an article on some of the replications of the Minneapolis experiment on police responses to spouse abuse by suggesting that "deterrence may be effective for a substantial segment of the offender population....

However, the underlying mechanisms remain obscure". A new study could focus on the mechanisms: Why or under what conditions does the arrest of offenders who are employed deter them from future criminal acts? Exactly what occurs when someone is arrested for domestic violence that may lead him or her not to be violent against a spouse in the future? Is it the brute fear of being arrested and having to go to jail? Is it the fear that one's employer may find out and fire him or her? Is it the fear that members of the community may learn about the arrest and the offender doesn't want to lose his or her good standing in the neighborhood? Is it all of these?

Any issue of a journal in your field is likely to have comments that point toward unresolved issues. The primary source of research questions for many criminologists is criminological theory. As you will soon learn, criminological theory provides an explanation as to why crime occurs, or occurs in some places and under some conditions but not others. Theory, then, is a very rich source of research ideas.

Some researchers spend much of their careers conducting research intended to refine an answer to one central research question. For example, you may find rational choice theory to be a useful approach to understanding diverse forms of social behavior, like crime, because you think people do seem to make decisions on the basis of personal cost-benefit calculations. So you may ask whether rational choice theory can explain why some people commit crimes and others do not, or why some people decide to quit committing crimes while others continue their criminal ways.

Finally, some research questions have very pragmatic sources. You may focus on a research question posed by someone else because doing so seems to be to your professional or financial advantage. Some criminologists conduct research on specific questions posed by a funding source in what is termed a request for proposals (RFP). (Sometimes the acronym RFA is used, meaning request for applications.) Or you may learn that the public defenders in your city are curious as to whether they are more successful in getting their clients acquitted of a criminal charge than private lawyers.

Refining the Questions

As you have perhaps surmised by now, the problem is not so much coming up with interesting criminological questions for research as it is focusing on a problem of manageable size. Researchers may worry about staking a research project (and thereby a grant) on a particular problem and so address several research questions at once, often in a jumbled fashion. It may also seem risky to focus on a research question that may lead to results discrepant with our own cherished assumptions about the social world.

In addition, the prospective commitment of time and effort for some research questions may seem overwhelming, resulting in a certain degree of paralysis. The best way to avoid these problems is to develop the research question one bit at a time with a step-by-step strategy. Don't keep hoping that the perfect research question will just spring forth from your pen. Instead, develop a list of possible research questions as you go along.

Evaluating the Questions

In the third stage of selecting a criminological research question, you evaluate the best candidate against the criteria for good social research questions: feasibility given the time and resources available, social importance, and scientific relevance. The research question in the Minneapolis Domestic Violence Experiment, "Does the formal sanction of police arrest versus non-arrest inhibit domestic violence?", certainly meets the criteria of social importance and scientific relevance, but it would not be a feasible question for a student project because it would require you to try to get the cooperation of a police department.

You might instead ask the question "Do people (students) think that arrest will inhibit domestic violence?" This is a question that you could study with an on-campus survey. Or perhaps you could work out an arrangement with a local battered women's shelter to study the question

"What leads some women to call the police when they are the victims of domestic violence, and why do they sometimes not call?" A review of the literature, however, might convince you that this and other questions may not be scientifically relevant because they have been studied enough.

You must be able to conduct any study within the time frame and resources you have. If time is short, questions that involve long-term change may not be feasible-for example, "If a state has recently changed its law so that it now permits capital punishment for those convicted of murder, does it eventually see a reduction in the homicide rate over time?" This is an interesting and important question, but one that requires years of data collection and research. Another issue is what people or groups you can expect to gain access to.

Although well-experienced researchers may be granted access to police or correctional department files to do their research, less seasoned and well-known researchers or students may not be granted such access. It is also often difficult for even the most experienced of researchers to be given full access to the deliberations of a criminal jury. For someone interested in white-collar crime, recording the interactions that take place in corporate boardrooms may also be taboo.

Then you must consider whether you will have any additional resources, such as other researchers to collaborate with or research funds. Remember that there are severe limits on what one person can accomplish. On the other hand, you might work in an organization that collects data on employees, customers, or clients that are relevant to your research interests. Or you may be able to piggyback your research onto a larger research project. You also must be prepared to handle large amounts of quantitative data.

A computer and the skills to use it will be essential. Also take into account the constraints you face due to your schedule and other professional or personal commitments and obligations. The Minneapolis Domestic Violence Experiment shows how ambitious social research questions can be when a team of seasoned researchers secures the backing of influential groups. The project required hundreds of thousands of dollars, the collaboration of many social scientists and criminal justice personnel, and the volunteer efforts of 41 Minneapolis police officers.

Importance of Criminological Research

Criminological research is not a simple undertaking, so you must focus on a substantive area that you feel is important and that is either important to the discipline or important for public policy. You also need to feel personally motivated to carry out the study; there is little point in trying to answer a question that doesn't interest you. In addition, you should consider whether the research question is important to other people. Will an answer to the research question make a difference for society? Again, the Minneapolis Domestic Violence Experiment is an exemplary case. If that study showed that a certain type of police response to domestic violence reduced the risk of subsequent victimization, a great deal of future violence could be prevented. But clearly, criminology and criminal justice are not wanting for important research questions.

Social scientists deal with such important issues as the effect of get-tough "three strikes" laws, whether strict supervision of those on parole and probation is more successful than less strict (and less costly) supervision, whether the death penalty deters criminals, whether gangs or the drug trade contributed to the rise in youth violence, whether crime is more prevalent in the United States than in European countries, whether gun control legislation reduces violence-we could go on and on. Many criminological questions deal with very important and troubling issues for our society.

Every research question in criminology should be grounded in the existing empirical literature. By grounded we mean the research we do must be informed by what others before us have done on the topic. Whether you formulate a research question because you have been stimulated by an academic article or because you want to investigate a current public policy problem, you must turn to the criminological literature to find out what has already been learned about this question. Even if your research topic has already been investigated by someone else, that does not necessarily mean it would be a bad idea for you to do research on the issue.

It would be unreasonable to think of any criminological research question as being settled for all time. You can be sure that some prior study is relevant to almost any research question you can think of, and you can also think of better ways to do research than have been done in the past. For example, the Minneapolis experiment was built on a substantial body of contradictory theorizing about the impact of punishment on criminality. Deterrence theory predicted that because it was a more severe penalty, arrest would better deter individuals from repeat offenses than not arresting them. Labeling theory, on the other hand, predicted that arrest would make repeat offenses more likely because it would stigmatize offenders.

The researchers found one prior experimental study of this issue, but it was conducted with juveniles. Studies among adults and nonexperimental research had not yielded consistent findings about the effects of arrest on recidivism in domestic violence cases. Clearly, the Minneapolis researchers had good reason for another study. Prior research and theory also helped them develop the most effective research design.

Role of Criminological Theory

Criminological theory can be a rich source of research questions. What deserves more attention at this point is the larger role of theory in research. Criminological theories do many things:

— They help us explain or understand things like why some people commit crimes or more crimes than others; why some people quit and others continue; and what the expected effect of good families, harsh punishment, or other factors on crime might be.

— They help us make predictions about the criminological world: "What would be the expected effect on the homicide rate if we employed capital punishment rather than life imprisonment?" "What would be the effect on the rate of property crimes if unemployment were to substantially increase?"

— They help us organize and make sense of empirical findings in a discipline.

— They help guide research.

— They help guide public policy: "What should we do to reduce the level of domestic violence?"

Social scientists, such as criminologists, who connect their work to theories in their discipline can generate better ideas about what to look for in a study and develop conclusions with more implications for other research. Building and evaluating theory is therefore one of the most important objectives of a social science like criminology. For centuries, scholars have been interested in developing theories about crime and criminals.

Sometimes these theories involve very fanciful ideas that are not well developed or organized, whereas at other times they strike us as being very compelling and well organized. Theories usually contain what are called theoretical constructs. In criminology, these theoretical constructs describe what is important to look at to understand, explain, predict, and "do something about" crime. For example, an important theoretical construct in differential association theory is the notion of "definitions favorable and unfavorable to the violation of law." Theories usually link one or more theoretical constructs to others in what are called relationship statements.

Differential association theory, for example, would link the theoretical construct of favorable/unfavorable definitions to the theoretical construct of involvement in crime to argue: "As one is exposed to more definitions favorable to the violation of law relative to definitions unfavorable to the violation of law, the more one is at risk for criminal behavior." This is a relationship statement that links two theoretical constructs-it states that as exposure to definitions favorable to the law increase, the risk of crime also increases. This is essentially a hypothesis that the theory of differential association entertains-if the theory is true, then the expected relationship should be true. The purpose of much criminological research is to examine the truth value, or empirical validity, of such theoretical relationship statements or hypotheses.

Some criminological theories reflect a substantial body of research and the thinking of many social scientists; others are formulated in the course of one investigation. A few have been widely accepted, at least for a time; others are the subject of vigorous controversy, with frequent changes and refinements in response to criticism and new research. Most criminological research is guided by some theory, although the theory may be only partially developed in a particular study or may even be unrecognized by the researcher. When researchers are involved in conducting a research project or engrossed in writing a research report, they may easily lose sight of the larger picture.

It is easy to focus on accumulating or clarifying particular findings rather than considering how the study's findings fit into a more general understanding of the social world. Furthermore just as theory guides research, research findings also influence the development of theory. We can use the studies of the police response to domestic assault to illustrate the value of theory for social research. Even in this very concrete and practical matter, we must draw on social theories to understand how people act and what should be done about those actions. Consider the three action options that police officers have when they confront a domestic assault suspect.

Fellow officers might urge forced separation to achieve short-term peace; police trainers might prefer mediation to resolve the underlying dispute; feminist groups might urge arrest to protect the victim. None of these recommendations is really a theory, but each suggests a different perspective on crime and legal sanctions. The traditional police perspective sees domestic violence as a family matter that should not be the object of formal legal action. The preference for mediation reflects the view that domestic violence involves a family crisis that can be solved with special counseling.

The pro-arrest position views domestic violence as a crime as serious as that between strangers and favors arrest for its presumed deterrent effect. You will encounter these different perspectives if you read much of the literature on domestic violence, or even if you talk with your friends about it. As Figure 1 shows, each perspective reflects different assumptions about gender roles, about the sources of crime, and about the impact of punishment. In turn, these assumptions reflect different experiences with family conflict, police actions, and the legal system. What we believe about one crime and the appropriate response to it relates to a great many other ideas we have about the social world. Recognizing these relationships is a first step toward becoming a theoretically guided social researcher and a theoretically informed consumer of social research.

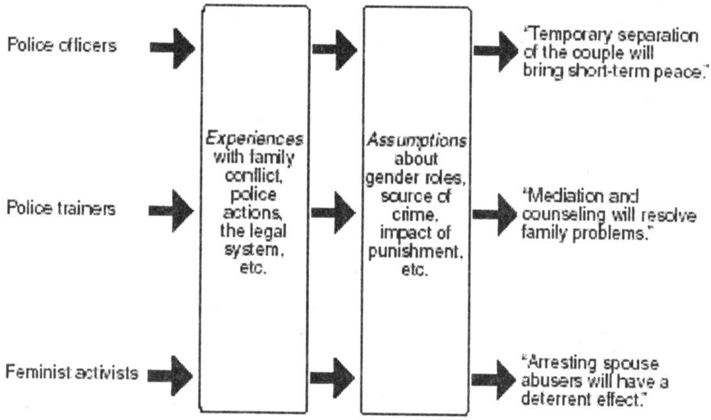

Figure 1. Bases for Three Perspectives on Intimate Partner Violence

Remember, however, that social theories do not provide the answers to the questions we confront as we formulate topics for research. Instead, social theories suggest the areas on which we should focus and the propositions that we should consider for a test. That is, theories suggest testable hypotheses about things and research verifies whether those hypotheses are true. In fact, one of the most important requirements of theory is that it be testable, or what philosophers of science call falsifiable-theoretical statements must be capable of being proven wrong.

If a body of thought cannot be empirically tested, it is more like philosophy than theory. For example, Sherman and Berk's domestic violence research was actually a test of predictions derived from two alternative theories of the impact of punishment on crime, deterrence theory and labeling theory: Deterrence theory presumes that human beings are at least marginally rational beings who are responsive to the expected costs and benefits of their actions. Committing a crime nets certain benefits for offenders; therefore, if we want to inhibit crime there must be a compensating cost-one cost is the criminal sanction (arrest, conviction, punishment).

Deterrence theory expects punishment to inhibit crime in two ways. General deterrence occurs when people see that crime results in undesirable punishments for others, that "crime doesn't pay." The persons who are punished serve as examples for those who have not yet committed an offense but might be thinking of what awaits them should they engage in proscribed acts. Specific deterrence occurs when persons who are punished decide not to commit another offense so they can avoid further punishment. Deterrence theory leads to the prediction that arresting spouse abusers will reduce the likelihood of their reoffending when compared with a less serious sanction (not being arrested but being warned or counseled).

Labeling theory distinguishes between primary deviance, the acts of individuals that lead to public sanction, and secondary deviance, the deviance that occurs in response to public sanction. Arrest or some other public sanction for misdeeds labels the offender as deviant in the eyes of others. Once the offender is labeled, others will treat the offender as a deviant, and he or she is then more likely to act in a way that is consistent with the deviant label. Ironically, the act of punishment stimulates more of the very behavior that it was intended to eliminate. This theory suggests that persons arrested for intimate partner violence are more likely to reoffend than those who are caught but not punished because the formal sanction of arrest is more stigmatizing than being warned or counseled. This prediction about the effect of formal legal sanctions is the reverse of the deterrence theory prediction.

Theorizing about the logic behind formal legal punishment also can help us draw connections to more general theories about social processes. Deterrence theory reflects the assumptions of rational choice theory, which assumes behavior is shaped by practical calculations: People break the law if the benefits of doing so exceed the costs. If crime is a rational choice for some people, then increasing the certainty or severity of punishment for crime should shift the cost-benefit balance away from criminal behavior.

Labeling theory is rooted in symbolic interactionism, which focuses on the symbolic meanings that people give to behavior. Instead of assuming that some forms of behavior are deviant in and of themselves, symbolic interactionists would view deviance as a consequence of the application of rules and sanctions to an offender. Figure 2 summarizes how these general theories relate to the question of whether to arrest spouse abusers.

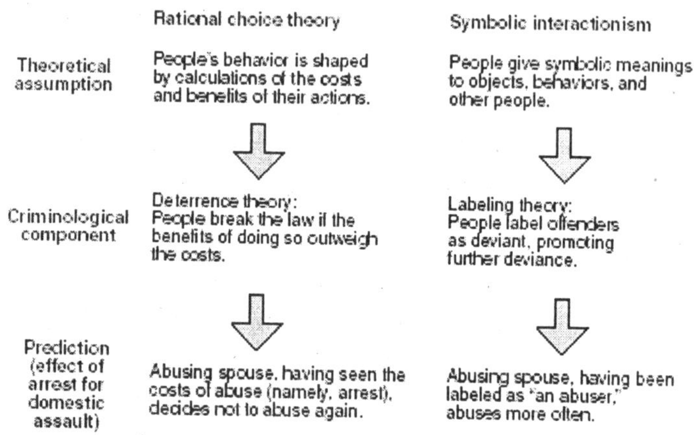

Figure 2. Two Social Theories and Their Predictions About the Effect of Arrest for Intimate Partner Assault

Does either deterrence theory or labeling theory make sense to you as an explanation for the impact of punishment? Do they seem consistent with your observations of social life? Over a decade after Sherman and Berk's study, Raymond Paternoster, Robert Brame, Ronet Bachman, and Lawrence Sherman decided to study punishment of domestic violence from a different perspective.

They turned to a social psychological theory called procedural justice theory, which explains law-abidingness as resulting from a sense of duty or morality. People obey the law from a sense of obligation that flows from seeing legal authorities as moral and legitimate. From this perspective, individuals who are arrested seem less likely to reoffend if they are treated fairly, irrespective of the outcome of their case, because fair treatment will enhance their view of legal authorities as moral and legitimate.

Procedural justice theory expands our view of the punishment process by focusing attention on how police act and how authorities treat subjects, rather than just on the legal decisions they make. Thus, it gives us a sense of the larger importance of the research question.

Are you now less certain about the likely effect of arrest for intimate partner violence? Will arrest decrease abuse because abusers do not wish to suffer from legal sanctions again? Will it increase abuse because abusers feel stigmatized by being arrested and thus are more likely to act like criminals? Or will arrest reduce abuse only if the abusers feel they have been treated fairly by the legal authorities? By suggesting such questions, social theory makes us much more sensitive to the possibilities and so helps us to design better research. Before, during, and after a research investigation, we need to keep thinking theoretically.

Social Research Strategies

All social research, including criminological research, is the effort to connect theory and empirical data, the evidence we find in the real world. As Figure 3 shows, theory and data have a two-way, mutually reinforcing relationship. Research that begins with a theory implying that certain data should be found involves deductive reasoning, which moves from general ideas (theory) to specific reality (data).

In contrast, inductive reasoning moves from the specific to the general. Both deductive reasoning and inductive reasoning are essential to criminologists. We cannot test an idea fairly unless we use deductive reasoning, stating our expectations in advance and setting up a test in which our idea could be shown to be wrong (falsified).

A theory that has not survived these kinds of tests can be regarded only as very tentative. Yet theories, no matter how cherished, cannot make useful predictions for every social situation or research problem that we seek to investigate. Moreover, we may find unexpected patterns in the data we collect, called serendipitous findings or anomalous findings. In either situation, we should reason inductively, making whatever theoretical sense we can of our unanticipated findings.

Research Circle

This process of conducting research, moving from theory to data and back again, or from data to theory and back again, can be characterized as a research circle. Figure 4 depicts this circle. Note that it mirrors the relationship between theory and data shown in Figure 3 and that it comprises three main research strategies: deductive research, inductive research, and descriptive research.

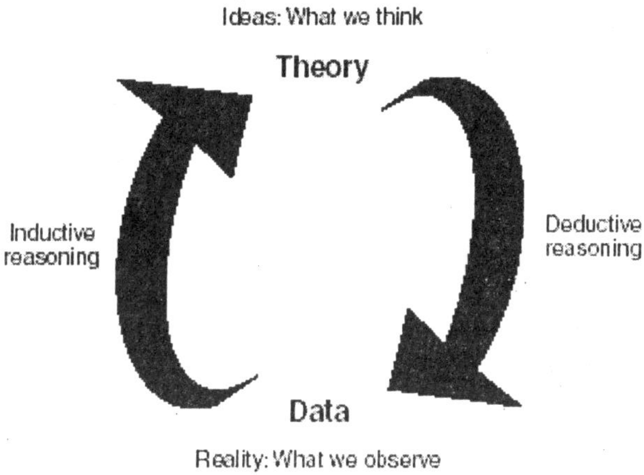

Figure 3. The Links Between Theory and Data

Deductive Research

As Figure 4 shows, deductive research proceeds from theorizing to data collection and then back to theorizing. In essence, a specific expectation is deduced from a general premise and then tested. Notice that a theory leads first to a hypothesis, which is a specific implication deduced from the more general theory. Researchers actually test a hypothesis, not the complete theory itself, because theories usually contain many hypotheses. A hypothesis proposes a relationship between two or more theoretical constructs or variables. Recall that a variable is a characteristic or property that can vary.

A constant is a characteristic or a property that cannot vary. For example, if we were to conduct some research in a male adult penitentiary, the theoretical construct "type of crime committed" would be a variable because persons will have been incarcerated for different offenses (one person is in for armed robbery, another for rape, etc.). However, the theoretical construct "gender" would be a constant because every inmate in the penitentiary would be male-gender does not vary, it is constant. Would age be a variable or a constant in this group? Would "criminal status" (offender or nonoffender) be a variable or a constant?

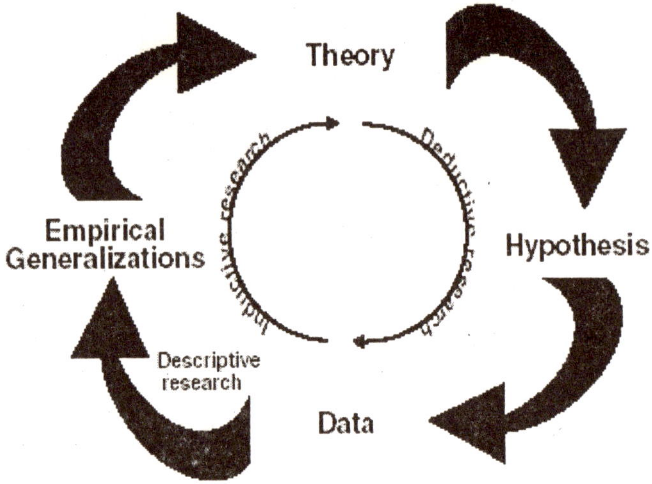

Figure 4. The Research Circle

Variables are of critical importance in research because in a hypothesis, variation in one variable is proposed to predict, influence, or cause variation in the other variable. The proposed influence is the independent variable; its effect or consequence is the dependent variable. After the researchers formulate one or more hypotheses and develop research procedures, they collect data with which to test the hypothesis.

Hypotheses can be worded in several different ways, and identifying the independent and dependent variables is sometimes difficult. When in doubt, try to rephrase the hypothesis as an if-then statement: "If the independent variable increases (or decreases), then the dependent variable increases (or decreases)." When researchers hypothesize that one variable increases as the other variable increases, Figure 5 Relationship Between Social Disorganization and Crime the direction of the association is positive (hypotheses 1 and 4 in the figure); when one variable decreases as the other variable decreases, the direction of association is also positive (hypothesis 3).

In positive relationships, then, the independent and dependent variables move in the same direction (as one increases, the other increases, or as one decreases, the other decreases). But when one variable increases as the other decreases, or vice versa, the direction of association is negative, or inverse (hypothesis 2). In a negative relationship, then, the independent and dependent variables move in opposite directions (as one increases, the other decreases, or as one decreases, the other increases). Hypothesis 5 is a special case, in which the independent variable is categorical. The independent variable cannot be said to increase or decrease. In this case, the concept of direction of association does not apply, and the hypothesis simply states that one category of the independent variable is associated with higher values on the dependent variable.

Figure 5 illustrates the hypothesis that social disorganization and a community's crime rate are positively related. The positive association implies that as social disorganization (the independent variable) increases (moves from being low to being high), the expected change is that the dependent variable will also increase (move from being low to high). This is the same thing as saying that as the level of social disorganization in a community moves from low to high, the level of crime also moves from low to high. In other words, the more social disorganization the more crime. Notice that in a positive relationship the independent and dependent variables are moving in the same direction-as social disorganization increases, so does crime. This positive relationship is shown in Figure 5 as an upward sloping line in the graph.

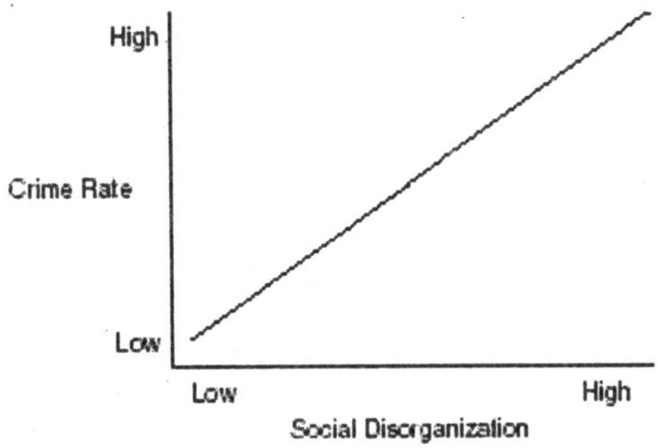

Figure 5. Relationship Between Social Disorganization and Crime

Figure 6 illustrates a graph for a negative association. This graph shows that as one's self-control becomes high, then the number of delinquent acts one commits declines or moves to low. This means that as self-control increases or strengthens, the frequency of delinquent behavior declines or decreases in number. Notice two things about this negative relationship. First, the independent and dependent variables move in opposite directions-as the independent variable (self-control) increases, the dependent variable (delinquency) decreases. Notice also that this negative relationship is shown as a downward sloping line in the graph.

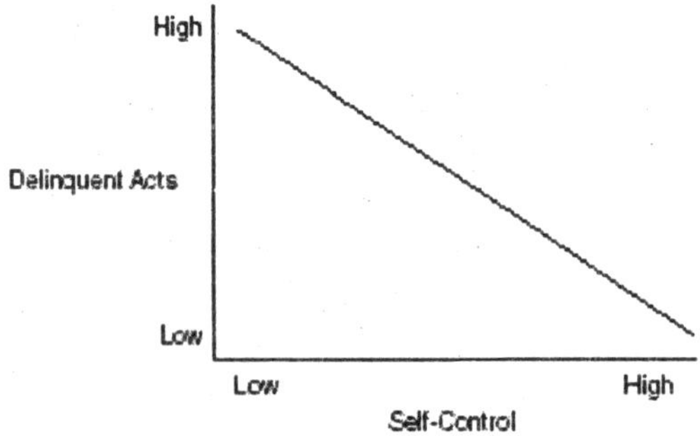

Figure 6. Relationship Between Self-Control and Number of Delinquent Acts

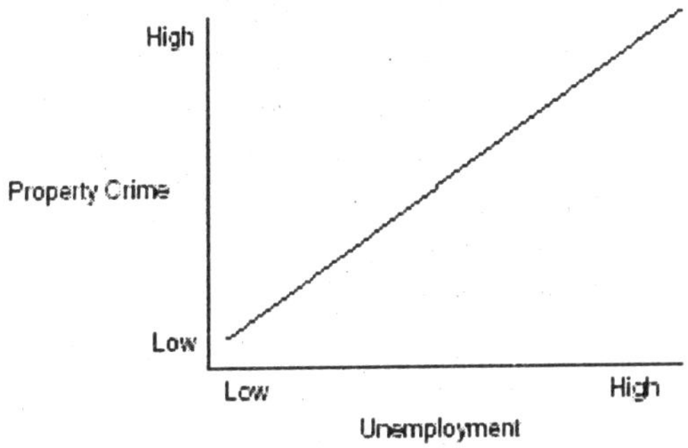

Figure 7. Relationship Between Unemployment and Property Crime

Figure 7 illustrates a positive relationship but the hypothesis is stated differently.

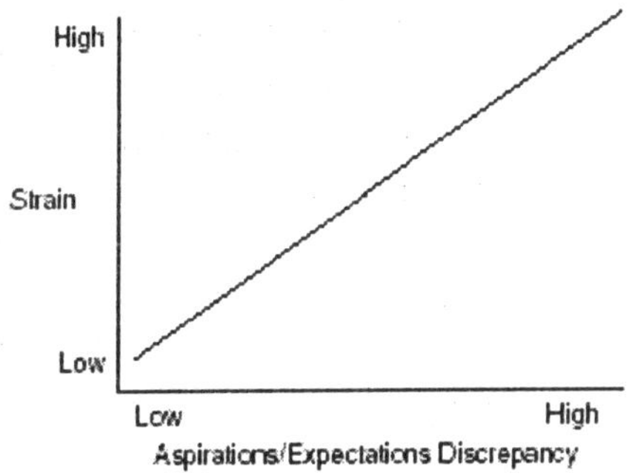

Figure 8. Relationship Between Aspirations/Expectations and Strain

Figure 9 illustrates a relationship with a graph that is slightly different from Figures 5 through 8. Here, the hypothesis states that we expect to see lower crime in communities that have foot patrols compared with communities that do not have foot patrols. Unlike the other independent variables, the independent variable foot patrol does not vary from low to high: Either there are foot patrols in the community or there are not.

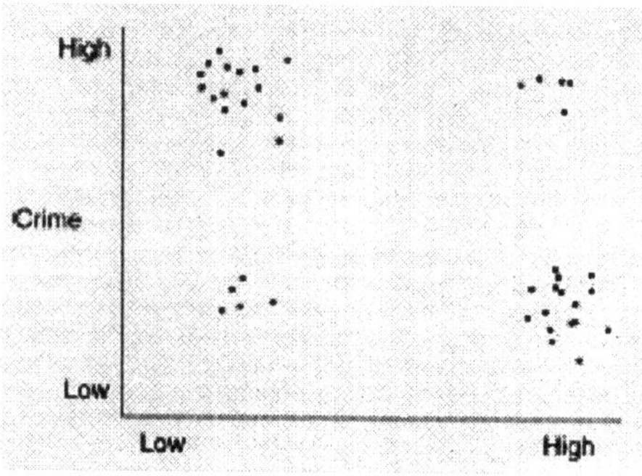

Figure 9. Relationship Between Foot Patrols and Crime

If the hypothesis is true, what we should expect to see is that most of the communities that do not have foot patrols should have high rates of crime, whereas most of those communities that do have foot patrols should have lower rates of crime. This expectation is shown in Figure 9 with the clump of points (representing communities) for the "no foot patrol" communities at the high range of crime and the clump of points for the "yes foot patrol" communities at the low range of crime.

The motives for deductive research include both explanation and evaluation. An example of explanatory deductive research is the Minneapolis Domestic Violence Experiment, in which Sherman and Berk sought to explain what sort of response by the authorities might keep a spouse abuser from repeating the offense. The researchers deduced from deterrence theory the expectation that arrest would deter domestic violence. They then collected data to test this expectation. The developers of the Second Step program had deduced from previous research in the violence prevention literature that violence in children could be inhibited if they learned and had practice with empathy, impulse control, and anger management.

Based on this trinity of approaches, Second Step was devised to reduce the expressed violence among those children in the program. Grossman and colleagues collected data to test this expectation. They did find that physically aggressive behavior was lower among those children in the program than among a comparable group not exposed to the curriculum. Even though they began not with an explicit theory of violence prevention but with a mass of previous research findings, the developers of the Second Step program did begin with some ideas about what would work in inhibiting the violent behavior of young children.

The evaluation by Grossman and his colleagues confirmed those ideas. In both explanatory and evaluative research, the statement of expectations for the findings and the design of the research to test these expectations strengthens the confidence we can place in the test. The deductive researcher shows her hand or states her expectations in advance and then designs a fair test of those expectations. Then "the chips fall where they may"; in other words, the researcher accepts the resulting data as a more or less objective picture of reality.

Inductive Research

In contrast to deductive research, inductive research begins at the bottom of the research circle and then works upward (Figure 4). The inductive researcher begins with specific data, which are then used to develop (induce) a general explanation (a theory) to account for the data. The patterns in the data are then summarized in one or more empirical generalizations that can be compared to the hypothesis. If the empirical generalizations are those stated in the hypothesis, then the theory from which the hypothesis was deduced is supported. If the empirical generalizations are inconsistent with the hypothesis, then the theory is not supported.

The motive for inductive research is exploration. The incident took place at a public university where a gunman tried to shoot the students in his class. Fortunately, the gun jammed, and all the students escaped uninjured. Because there was very little previous work in this area, Asmussen and Creswell conducted in-depth interviews with the students and tried to classify typical responses to the situation. Although the researchers did not develop a theory from their work, they did develop a classification scheme or taxonomy of different responses to traumatic events.

In strictly inductive research, the researcher already knows what he has found when he starts theorizing, or attempting to explain what accounts for these findings. The result can be new insights and provocative questions. But the adequacy of an explanation formulated after the fact is necessarily less certain than an explanation presented prior to the collection of data. Every phenomenon can always be explained in some way. Inductive explanations are thus more trustworthy if they are tested subsequently with deductive research.

Qualitative research is often inductive: The researchers begin by observing social interaction or interviewing social actors in depth and then developing an explanation for what has been found. The researchers often ask questions like "What is going on here?" "How do people interpret these experiences?" or "Why do people do what they do?" Rather than testing a hypothesis, the researchers are trying to make sense of some social phenomenon. Lauren Bennett, Lisa Goodman, and Mary Ann Dutton used this approach to investigate one of the problems that emerge when police arrest domestic batterers: The victims often decide not to press charges. Bennett et al. did not set out to test hypotheses with qualitative interviews (there was another, hypothesis-testing component in their research), but sought, inductively, to "add the voice of the victim to the discussion" and present "themes that emerged from the interviews."

Descriptive Research

Descriptive research can be considered a part of the research circle, even though such research does not involve connecting theory and data. As Figure 4 indicates, descriptive research starts with data and proceeds only to the stage of making empirical generalizations based on those data. Valid description is important in its own right, but it is also critical in all research. Description of social phenomena can stimulate more ambitious deductive and inductive research.

The Minneapolis Domestic Violence Experiment was motivated in part by a growing body of descriptive research indicating that spouse abuse is very common. The Youth Risk Behavior Survey is an ongoing study that attempts to measure the involvement of a national sample of youth in a wide sweep of antisocial behaviors. This descriptive work is valuable in documenting patterns and trends in violence by American youth throughout the 1990s. Theories will then be developed to account for these patterns and trends.

Domestic Violence

The Sherman and Berk study of domestic violence is a good example of how the research circle works. In an attempt to determine ways to prevent the recurrence of spouse abuse, the researchers repeatedly linked theory and data, developing both hypotheses and empirical generalizations.

Phase 1: Deductive research

The first phase of Sherman and Berk's study was designed to test a hypothesis. According to deterrence theory, punishment will reduce recidivism, or the propensity to commit further crimes. From this theory, Sherman and

Berk deduced a specific hypothesis: "Arrest for spouse abuse reduces the risk of repeat offenses." In this hypothesis, arrest is the independent variable, and variation in the risk of repeat offenses is the dependent variable (it is hypothesized to depend on arrest).

Of course, in another study arrest might be the dependent variable in relation to some other independent variable. For example, in the hypothesis "The greater the rate of layoffs in a community, the higher the frequency of arrest," the dependent variable is frequency of arrest. Only within the context of a hypothesis, or a relationship between variables, does it make sense to refer to one variable as dependent and the other as independent. Sherman and Berk tested their hypothesis by setting up an experiment in which the police responded to complaints of spouse abuse in one of three ways, one of which was to arrest the offender.

When the researchers examined their data (police records for the persons in their experiment), they found that of those arrested for assaulting their spouse, only 13% repeated the offense, compared to a 26% recidivism rate for those who were separated from their spouse by the police without any arrest. This pattern in the data, or empirical generalization, was consistent with the some discrepancies troubled critics. The generalizability of the study's results was the researchers' greatest concern. Minneapolis is no more a typical U.S. city than any other, and we cannot assume that police policies that are effective in Minneapolis will be equally effective in cities with very different political histories, criminal justice agencies, and population characteristics.

Sherman and Berk warned readers, "External validity will have to wait for replications"; that is, for repetitions of the study using the same research methods to answer the same research question. Finally, Sherman and Berk's claims about the causal validity of their results rested primarily on the experimental design they used. The 330 domestic assault cases in the study were handled by the police in one of three ways: an arrest, an order that the offending spouse leave the house for 8 hours, or some type of verbal advice by the police officers.

The officers were not allowed to choose which treatment to apply (except in extreme cases, such as when severe injury had occurred or when the spouse had demanded that an arrest be made). Instead, the treatments were carried out by police in random order, according to the color of the next report form on a pad that had been prepared by the researchers.

By insisting on the random assignment of cases to treatments, the researchers tried to ensure that police officers would not arrest just the toughest spouses or the spouses who seemed most obnoxious or the spouses they encountered late in the day. In other words, the random assignment procedure made it unlikely that arrested spouse abusers would differ, on average, from the other spouse abusers except for the fact that they were arrested (although, because of chance factors, the possibility of other differences cannot be completely ruled out). The researchers' conclusion that arrest caused a lower incidence of repeat offenses therefore seems valid.

Phase 2: Deductive research

Because of their doubts about the generalizability of their results, Sherman, Berk, and new collaborators began to journey around the research circle again, with funding from the National Institute of Justice for replications (repetitions) of the experiment in six more cities. These replications used the same basic research approach but with some improvements. The random assignment process was tightened up in most of the cities so that police officers would be less likely to replace the assigned treatment with a treatment of their own choice.

In addition, data were collected about repeat violence against other victims as well as against the original complainant. Some replications also examined different aspects of the arrest process, to see whether professional counseling helped and whether the length of time spent in jail after arrest mattered at all. By the time results were reported from five of the cities in the new study, a problem was apparent. In three cities-Omaha, Nebraska; Charlotte, North Carolina; and Milwaukee, Wisconsin-researchers were finding long-term increases in domestic violence incidents among arrestees. But in Colorado Springs, Colorado, and Dade County, Florida, the predicted deterrent effects seemed to be occurring.

Sherman and his colleagues had now traversed the research circle twice in an attempt to answer the original research question, first in Minneapolis and then in six other cities. But rather than leading to more confidence in deterrence theory, the research results were calling it into question. Deterrence theory now seemed inadequate to explain empirical reality, at least as the researchers had measured this reality. So the researchers began to reanalyze the follow-up data from several cities to try to explain the discrepant results, thereby starting around the research circle once again.

Phase 3: Inductive research

At this point, the researchers' approach became more inductive, and they began trying to make sense of the differing patterns in the data collected in the different cities. Could systematic differences in the samples or in the implementation of arrest policies explain the differing outcomes? Or was the problem an inadequacy in the theoretical basis of their research? Was deterrence theory really the best way to explain the patterns in the data they were collecting? Sherman and his colleagues now turned to control theory, yet another broad explanation for social behavior. It predicts that having a stake in conformity (resulting from inclusion in social networks at work or in the community) decreases a person's likelihood of committing crimes.

The implication is that people who are employed and married are more likely to be deterred by the threat of arrest than those without such stakes in conformity. This is because an arrest for domestic violence could jeopardize one's job and one's marriage, thus making arrest more costly for the employed and married. This is indeed what a reexamination of the data revealed: Individuals who were married and employed were deterred from repeat offenses by arrest, but individuals who were unmarried and unemployed were actually more likely to commit repeat offenses if they were arrested. This was an important theoretical insight, for it suggested that one powerful way that formal sanctions work is that they can potentially trigger informal sanctions or costs (e.g., loss of respect from friends and family).

Now the researchers had traversed the research circle almost three times, a process perhaps better described as a spiral (Figure 11). The first two times the researchers had traversed the research circle in a deductive, hypothesis-testing way: They started with theory and then deduced and tested hypotheses. The third time they traversed the research circle in a more inductive, exploratory way: They started with empirical generalizations from the data they had already obtained and then turned to a new theory to account for the unexpected patterns in the data. At this point they believed that deterrence theory makes correct predictions given certain conditions and that another theory, control theory, may specify what these conditions are.

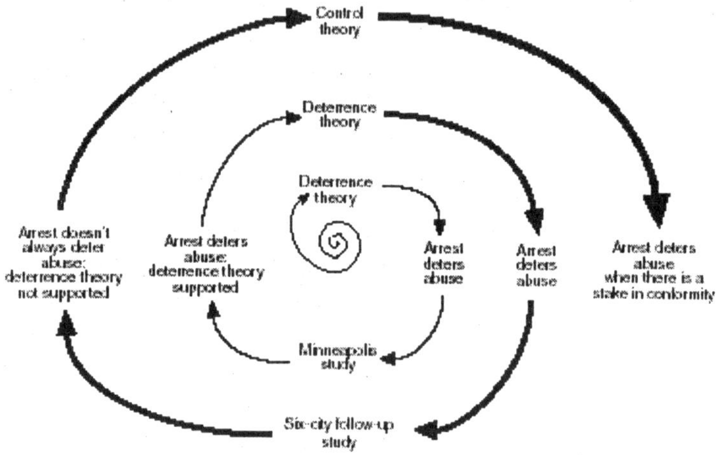

Figure 11. The Research Spiral: Minneapolis Domestic Violence Experiment

After two and one-half cycles through the research circle, the picture became more complex but also conceptually richer. The researchers came closer to understanding how to inhibit domestic violence. But they cautioned us that their initial question-the research problem-was still not completely answered. Employment status and marital status alone do not measure the strength of social attachments; they also are related to how much people earn and the social standing of victims in court. So perhaps social ties are not really what make arrest an effective deterrent to domestic violence. The real deterrent may be cost-benefit calculations or perceptions about the actions of authorities. More research was still needed.

Phase 4: Deductive research

In 1997, Paternoster, Sherman, and two other criminologists reexamined data from the Milwaukee Domestic Violence Experiment to test hypotheses derived from yet another theory, procedural justice theory. Procedural justice theory predicts that people will comply with the law out of a sense of duty and obligation if they are treated fairly by legal authorities. In the Milwaukee sample, arrest had a criminogenic effect: Those who were arrested were subsequently more likely to abuse their spouses than those who were simply warned. Paternoster and his colleagues thought that this effect might have been due to the way subjects were treated when they were arrested rather than simply to the fact that they were arrested.

One of their hypotheses spells out the reasoning. Among those persons arrested for spouse assault, those who perceive themselves as being treated in a procedurally unfair manner will be more likely to commit acts of spouse assault in the future than those arrested persons who perceive themselves as being treated in a procedurally fair manner, net of other determinants of violence. To carry out this study, Paternoster and his colleagues reexamined data collected earlier in Milwaukee, where the findings had seemed anomalous. However, this reanalysis of the data qualifies as deductive research, because the hypotheses were derived from theory and then tested with the data, rather than being induced by the data.

The procedural justice hypotheses were supported: Persons who were arrested in the Milwaukee experiment became more likely to reoffend only if they perceived that they had been treated unfairly by the police. Otherwise, their rate of rearrest was similar to that for the persons who were not arrested. Thus, another element was added to our understanding of the effects of the police response to domestic violence.

Clearly our understanding of effective responses to domestic violence will never truly be complete, but research to date has greatly improved our understanding of this social problem. The future should yield an even better understanding, even though at times it may be hard to make sense out of conflicting findings from different studies. Science is an ongoing enterprise in which findings cumulate and eventually yield greater understanding or even radical revisions in our understanding. Needless to say, researchers don't need to worry about running out of work to do.

16

Guidelines for Criminological Researchers

Any effort to understand the social world is plagued by pitfalls, including such everyday errors in reasoning as overgeneralization, selective or inaccurate observation, illogical reasoning, and resistance to change. Social scientists, including criminologists, cannot avoid these problems entirely, but they try to minimize their impact by adhering to certain guidelines. The guidelines followed by social researchers fall into two categories: those that help keep research scientific and those that help keep research ethical. Both types of guidelines are essential for a field of inquiry that seeks empirical generalizations about human society. To point out their value, we'll use some examples from the domestic violence research.

Scientific Guidelines

The following nine guidelines are applicable to any type of scientific research, but they are particularly useful to criminologists and to those who read about criminology and criminal justice. Adherence to these guidelines will reduce the temptation "to project on what is observed whatever [they] want the world to be for [their] own private purposes".

1. *Test ideas against empirical reality without becoming too personally invested in a particular outcome*: This testing approach is reflected in the research process and is implicit in the goal of validity. It contrasts markedly with our everyday methods of figuring things out, in which we typically just react to events as they happen, without paying much attention to whether we really are putting our ideas to a test. Empirical testing requires a neutral and open-minded approach: The scientists are personally disinterested in the outcome and not swayed by the popularity or the social status of those who would prefer other outcomes. This does not mean that the researchers are not personally involved or interested in the research-they must be-rather, the point is that they cannot have so much invested in a research project personally or professionally that they try in subtle or not-so-subtle ways to affect the outcome.

2. *Plan and carry out investigations systematically*: Social researchers have little hope of conducting a careful test of their ideas if they do not think through in advance how they should go about the test and then proceed accordingly. But a systematic approach is not always easy. For example, Sherman and Berk needed to ensure that spouse abusers were assigned to be either arrested or not on a random basis, rather than on the basis of the police officers' personal preferences. So the researchers devised an elaborate procedure using randomly sequenced report sheets in different colors. But the researchers found that police officers did not always follow this systematic procedure. Subsequently, in some replications of the study, the researchers ensured compliance with their research procedures by requiring police officers to call in to a central number to receive the experimentally determined treatment.

3. *Document all procedures, and disclose them publicly*: Social researchers who disclose the methods on which their conclusions rest allow others to evaluate for themselves the likely soundness of these conclusions. Such disclosure is a key feature of science. Again, Sherman and Berk provide a compelling example. In their research report, after describing the formal research plan, they describe at length the apparent slippage from this plan, which occurred primarily because some police officers avoided implementing the random assignment procedure.

4. *Clarify assumptions*: No investigation is complete unto itself; whatever the researcher's method, the research rests on some background assumptions. Research to determine whether arrest has a deterrent effect assumes that potential law violators think rationally-that they calculate potential costs and benefits prior to committing crimes. When a researcher conducts an election poll, the assumption is that people actually vote for the candidate they say they will vote for. When government unemployment statistics are used to describe the state of the economy, the assumption is that those statistics reflect actual fluctuations in unemployment. By definition, research assumptions are not tested, so we do not know whether they are correct. In fact, researchers themselves do not always recognize the assumptions they are making. By taking the time to think about and to disclose their assumptions, researchers provide important information for those who seek to evaluate the validity of their conclusions.

5. *Specify the meaning of all terms*: Words often have multiple or unclear meanings. Strain, differential association, social disorganization, subculture of violence, problemoriented policing, and so on can mean different things to different people. Thus the

terms used in scientific research must be defined explicitly and used consistently. For example, Sherman and Berk identified their focus as misdemeanor domestic assault, not just wife beating. They specified that their work concerned those cases of domestic assault in which severe injury was not involved and both partners were present when police arrived.

6. *Maintain a skeptical stance toward current knowledge*: Scientists may feel very confident about interpretations of the social or natural world that have been supported by repeated investigations, but the results of any particular investigation must be examined critically. A general skepticism about current knowledge stimulates researchers to improve the validity of current research results and expand the frontier of knowledge. For example, in response to questions raised about the Sherman and Berk study, Lawrence Sherman and Ellen Cohn discussed 13 problems of the Minneapolis Domestic Violence Experiment in a published critique, weighing carefully the extent to which these problems might have affected its validity. This critique could then stimulate additional research designed to address the problematic aspects of the original research.

7. *Replicate research and accumulate knowledge*: No one study can be viewed as definitive in itself; usually at least some plausible threats to the validity of the conclusions exist. And no conclusion can be understood adequately apart from the larger body of knowledge to which the study is related. Scientific investigations may begin with a half-baked or off-the-wall idea, but a search of the literature for other relevant work must be conducted in short order. The other side of the coin is that the results of scientific research must be published, to serve as a foundation for others who seek to replicate or extend the research.

Sherman reported that when he and his colleagues decided to attempt some replications of their own experiment, they found that another research team was already planning to do so. The process of extending knowledge gained in the Minneapolis experiment had already begun.

8. *Maintain an interest in theory*: Theories organize the knowledge accumulated by numerous investigations into a coherent whole and serve as a guide to future inquiries. Even though much research is purely descriptive, this research can still serve as a basis for others to evaluate different theories. The Minneapolis Domestic Violence Experiment was devised initially as a test of the competing predictions of deterrence and labeling theory, but the researchers extended their attention to control theory to help them explain unanticipated findings. These theoretical connections make the research much more relevant to other criminologists working to understand different types of crime and social control.

9. *Search for regularities or patterns*: Science is concerned with classes rather than with individuals (except inasmuch as individuals are representatives of a class). Scientists assume that the natural world has some underlying order of relationships, and that every event and individual is not so unique that general principles cannot be discerned. Individuals are not unimportant to criminologists and other social scientists; Sherman, for example, described the abuse histories of two men to provide greater insight into why arrest could have different effects for different people. But the goal of elaborating individual cases is to understand social patterns that characterize many individuals.

These general guidelines are only ideals for social research. No particular investigation is going to follow every guideline exactly. Real investigations by criminologists do not always include much attention to theory, specific definitions of all terms, and so forth. But any study that strays far from these guidelines cannot be considered scientific.

Ethical Guidelines

Every scientific investigation, whether in the natural sciences or in the social sciences, such as criminology and criminal justice, has an ethical dimension. First and foremost, the scientific concern with validity requires that scientists be honest and reveal their methods. (How else could we determine whether the requirement of honesty has been met?) Scientists also have to consider the uses to which their findings will be put. In addition, because criminological research deals with people, such as criminals, criminal suspects, and incarcerated inmates, and controversial topics (involvement in crime), criminologists have some unique ethical concerns.

Research distorted by political or personal pressures to find particular outcomes or to achieve the most marketable results is unlikely to be carried out in an honest and open fashion or to achieve valid results. For example, noted English biologist Sir Cyril Burt published fabricated evidence in 1961 that purported to show intelligence is determined primarily by heredity. In the 35 years before Burt's deliberate falsification was exposed, his study influenced much social science theory and research (and was in part responsible for Burt's knighthood. Efforts to evaluate the influence of inherited characteristics on people were considerably set back by this fraud. Being open about one's research is particularly important when the research is used or influential in public policy matters.

For example, an economist, Isaac Ehrlich, who was interested in the study of crime conducted a study that examined whether capital punishment deters murder.

Using national data for the time period 1933-1969, Ehrlich concluded that each execution prevented or deterred 7-8 homicides-in other words, Ehrlich claimed that executions saved 7-8 innocent crime victims. This was one of a very few studies at the time to find a deterrent effect for capital punishment. In fact, his results were cited in a U.S. Supreme Court case (Gregg v. Georgia) as evidence in support of deterrence. His reported findings caused both a stir among proponents of capital punishment and skeptical hostility among its critics. Other researchers immediately wanted to reexamine Ehrlich's data to see how valid his results were. Unfortunately, Professor Ehrlich was not immediately forthcoming with his data.

The controversy surrounding his findings grew when other researchers tried to duplicate his findings with data they collected and found that when they analyzed slightly different years, with slightly different variables and sometimes slightly different statistical strategies, the effect of executions changed. In some analyses, executions seemed to deter murder; in some others, it seemed to increase murders (what was called a brutalization effect); and in others it had no discernable effect at all. The controversy about Ehrlich's findings bubbled for years and might have been resolved much sooner had Professor Ehrlich been more open and forthcoming about his data. Openness about research procedures and results goes hand in hand with honesty in research design. Openness is also essential if researchers are to learn from the work of others.

In spite of this need for openness, some researchers may hesitate to disclose their procedures or results to prevent others from building on their ideas and taking some of the credit. You may have heard of the long legal battle between a U.S. researcher and a French researcher about how credit should be allocated for discovering the AIDS virus. Although such public disputes are unusual, concerns with priority of discovery are common. Scientists are like other people in their desire to be first. Enforcing standards of honesty and encouraging openness about research is the best solution for these problems.

The Use of Science

Scientists must also consider the extent to which they should publicize their research and the uses to which it is put. Although many scientists believe that personal values should be left outside the laboratory, some argue that it is proper, even desirable, for scientists in their role as citizens to attempt to influence public policy. In other words, if their research has something to say about how things should be done, some scientists feel that they should actively promote their work. Sometimes, however, there is controversy on this point.

Sherman and Berk were criticized by other scholars on the basis that the findings of one study are not a sufficient empirical base on which to draw such an important public policy recommendation. In fact, Sherman and Berk did caution that their findings might not be replicated in other locations, and that their position is that police should be able to arrest domestic violence suspects, not that they should be required to. Nevertheless, because Sherman publicized the results of the research in the mass media, he was criticized by some social scientists for implicitly encouraging police departments to change their policies on the basis of preliminary evidence (the results of just one study in one city).

In part, the question was whether basing policy on partial information was preferable to waiting until the information was more complete (more studies conducted in different locations). Sherman later pointed out that in the Omaha follow-up study, arrest warrants were very effective in reducing repeat offenses among spouse abusers who had already left the scene when police arrived at the time of the initial complaint. Absent offenders had not been included in the initial study, and because the Omaha finding was not publicized, it did not become known to police chiefs or battered women's groups.

As a consequence, Sherman suggested, some domestic violence that might have been prevented was not prevented. How much publicity is warranted, and at what point in the research is it warranted? He also argued that public policy is better guided by partial knowledge than no knowledge at all. Criminologists who conduct research on behalf of organizations and agencies may face additional difficulties. When an organization contracts with a researcher to evaluate a program, identify community needs, or explore product potential, usually the organization, not the researcher, controls the final report and the publicity it receives.

If organizational leaders decide that particular research results are inconsistent with their funding requests, community image, or employee relations, they may refuse to release the results or require changes that the researcher deems unacceptable. In a situation like this, a researcher's desire to have findings used appropriately and reported fully can conflict with contractual obligations. Researchers often can anticipate such dilemmas in advance and resolve them when the contract for research is negotiated, or decline a particular research opportunity altogether if acceptable terms cannot be worked out. But often these problems come up after a report has been drafted, when the researcher finds out that the report is unacceptable to a top-level administrator or executive whom the researcher does not even know.

In addition, a researcher's need to have a job or to maintain particular personal relationships may make it difficult to act in what the researcher thinks is the most ethical manner. A way to minimize these possibilities is to acknowledge the source of research funding in reports and to carefully scrutinize those research reports funded by organizations or agencies with a stake in the outcome.

Research on Human

In physics or chemistry, research subjects (objects and substances) may be treated to extreme conditions and then discarded when they are no longer useful. However, social (and medical) scientists must concern themselves with the way their human subjects are treated in the course of research. This treatment may involve manipulations and deceptions in laboratory experiments, sensitive questions in survey research, observations in field studies, or analyses of personal data.

Contemporary standards for the treatment of human subjects are set by the federal government, by professional associations, by special university review boards, and in some cases by ethics committees in other organizations. Federal regulations require that the proposals of researchers seeking federal funds for research on human subjects be reviewed by an institutional review board (IRB) before they are submitted for federal review. IRBs at universities and other agencies in turn apply ethics standards set by government agencies, like the National Institutes of Health, and may develop more specific guidelines of their own.

The American Society of Criminology (ASC), one of criminology's professional organizations, is in the process of redrafting their code of ethics, but advises members to seek guidance from similar organizations including the American Sociological Association (ASA). The ASA's standards concerning the treatment of human subjects include federal regulations and ethics guidelines emphasized by most professional social science organizations:

- Research should cause no harm to subjects.
- Participation in research should be voluntary, and therefore subjects must give their informed consent to participate in the research.
- Researchers should fully disclose their identity.
- Anonymity or confidentiality must be maintained for individual research participants, unless it is voluntarily and explicitly waived.
- The benefits of a research project should outweigh any foreseeable risks.

Index